USAF WARRIOR STUDIES

Richard H. Kohn and Joseph P. Harahan
General Editors

AIR SUPERIORITY
IN
WORLD WAR II AND KOREA

An interview with Gen. James Ferguson,
Gen. Robert M. Lee, Gen. William Momyer,
and Lt. Gen. Elwood R. Quesada

Edited with an introduction
by Richard H. Kohn and
Joseph P. Harahan

OFFICE OF AIR FORCE HISTORY
UNITED STATES AIR FORCE
WASHINGTON, D.C. 1983

Library of Congress Cataloging in Publication Data

Main entry under title:

Air superiority in World War II and Korea.

(USAF warrior studies)
Includes bibliographical references and index.
1. World War, 1939-1945—Aerial operations, American.
2. Korean War, 1950–1953—Aerial operations, American.
3. Air power.
4. Generals—United States—Interviews.
I. Kohn, Richard H.
II. Harahan, Joseph P. III. United
States. Air Force. Office of Air Force History.
IV. Series.
D790.A73 1983   940.54'4973   83-2436

ISBN 0-912799-00-5

Project Warrior Studies are published by the Office of Air Force History. The views expressed in this publication are those of the interview participants and do not necessarily reflect the policies of the United States Air Force or the Department of Defense.

For sale by the Superintendent of Documents, U.S. Government Printing Office
Washington, D.C. 20402

Foreword

The publication of *Air Superiority in World War II and Korea* is part of a continuing series of historical studies from the Office of Air Force History in support of Project Warrior.

Project Warrior seeks to create and maintain within the Air Force an environment where Air Force people at all levels can learn from the past and apply the warfighting experiences of past generations to the present. When Gen. Lew Allen, Jr., initiated the project in 1982, he called for the "continuing study of military history, combat leadership, the principles of war and, particularly, the applications of air power." All of us in the Air Force community can benefit from such study and reflection. The challenges of today and the future demand no less.

CHARLES A. GABRIEL, General, USAF
Chief of Staff

United States Air Force
Historical Advisory Committee
(As of May 1, 1983)

Lt. Gen. Charles G. Cleveland, USAF
Commander, Air University, ATC

Mr. DeWitt S. Copp
The National Volunteer Agency

Dr. Warren W. Hassler, Jr.
Pennsylvania State University

Dr. Edward L. Homze
University of Nebraska

Dr. Alfred F. Hurley
Brig. Gen., USAF, Retired
North Texas State University

Maj. Gen. Robert E. Kelley, USAF
Superintendent, USAF Academy

Dr. Joan Kennedy Kinnaird
Trinity College

Mr. David E. Place,
The General Counsel, USAF

Gen. Bryce Poe II,
USAF, Retired

Dr. David A. Shannon (*Chairman*)
University of Virginia

Contents

Photographs

Maps

Introduction

In November 1981, Lt. Gen. Hans H. Driessnack, Assistant Vice Chief of Staff, asked the Historical Program to assemble a small number of retired officers for a group oral history interview. General Driessnack believed that in reminiscing together, these officers would recall incidents and experiences that might otherwise go unrecorded; by exchanging ideas and questioning each other—in effect, interviewing each other—they would recall material that would be of interest and importance to the Air Force today. General Driessnack also suggested selecting retired officers from the senior statesman conference, a gathering every spring at which retired four-star generals are briefed on Air Force issues and then discuss them with contemporary Air Force leaders.

The result is the following interview. The four participants—Gen. James Ferguson, Gen. Robert M. Lee, Gen. William W. Momyer, and Lt. Gen. Elwood R. "Pete" Quesada—gathered on May 21, 1982, around a table in the Vandenberg room at the Bolling Air Force Base Officers' Club. For approximately two and one half hours they responded to questions sent to them earlier and discussed air superiority in World War II and Korea. Their discussions ranged far and wide: flying in the pre-World War II Army Air Corps, campaigning in North Africa and Western Europe in World War II, planning and participating in the Normandy invasion, using secret intelligence supplied by Ultra, struggling to codify tactical air doctrine in the postwar years, fighting the air battle in Korea, and thinking about the general problem of air superiority throughout their careers. This collective interview is not history but the source material on which history rests; it is a memoir, a first-hand account by air leaders who flew, fought, and commanded tactical air forces in combat.

Combat memoirs are usually exciting, vivid, and filled with colorful anecdotes. That is true for this oral interview, except that the discussions are focused on only one topic: air superiority. The Historical Program chose air superiority because it is a crucial first element in all air operations and because it seemed to be neglected by a military establishment that so

1

quickly dominated enemy air forces in the last two wars. There is a need to know more about air superiority: what it means, when it is necessary, and how it can be achieved operationally when the airspace is contested. The careers of each of the participants reveal a long association with air superiority—the theories and operations.

General James Ferguson was born in Smyrna, Turkey, and raised in Scotland and California. In 1934 he enlisted in the Army Air Corps as a flying cadet and learned to fly a variety of attack and pursuit aircraft. Ferguson entered World War II as a lieutenant. During the war, he successively commanded a pursuit squadron (79th), a pursuit group (20th), a fighter group (337th), and a fighter-bomber group (405th). He saw action in Normandy, western France, Belgium, and Germany. Two months prior to the June 1944 Normandy invasion, he became assistant chief of staff in Brig. Gen. "Pete" Quesada's IX Fighter Command. During the invasion, General Quesada sent Ferguson to France to act as a forward air controller directing fighter aircraft in close air support missions. He remained in France throughout the invasion and breakout battles, helping direct the IX Fighter Command's 1,500 aircraft in close air support, interdiction, and reconnaissance missions. During the crucial battle for Normandy and for all of June 1944, the command flew 30,863 sorties, dropped 7,366 tons of bombs, and destroyed German aircraft, bridges, trains, locomotives, rolling stock, tanks, and army motor vehicles. As the fighting continued across France and into Germany, General Ferguson compiled an extensive air combat record. For his World War II service, he received a Distinguished Service Medal, three Legions of Merit, two Air Medals, and similar honors from Allied nations. Following a brief stint in the Pacific theater, he returned to the United States in 1946 and began teaching tactical air concepts and doctrines at the Air Command and Staff School at Maxwell Field, Alabama.

When North Korean forces invaded South Korea on June 25, 1950, General Ferguson was in Japan, having just been reassigned a few weeks before to the USAF Far East Air Forces. Within a year he became vice commander of the Fifth Air Force, the tactical air force supporting the U.S. Eighth Army, the American army in Korea. In that capacity he worked with Gen. Frank F. Everest, Fifth Air Force commander, and Gen. Otto P. Weyland, commander of the Far East Air Forces, in developing operational plans for a sustained interdiction campaign against the North Korean railheads and rail system. When challenged by the Chinese Communist Air Force equipped with Mig–15 fighters, the Fifth Air Force responded with F–86 Sabre jets. An intensive air battle for control of North Korean airspace resulted in a decisive victory for the American jets.

General Ferguson's post-Korean war assignments centered on guiding research and development of new fighter aircraft and tactical missiles. In 1961 he became the deputy chief of staff for research and development, United States Air Force. He remained in that key job for five years and guided Air Force efforts in developing intercontinental ballistic missiles, strategic bombers, satellites, tactical fighters, and communications. In September 1966 General Ferguson became the commander of the Air Force Systems Command. He retired from that position in 1970.

On graduating from the United States Military Academy in 1931, Gen. Robert M. Lee was commissioned in the U.S. Cavalry.   Quickly transferring into the Army Air Corps, he learned to fly at Randolph and Kelly Fields, Texas. In 1937 he returned to the Army Cavalry (Mechanized) and progressed rapidly in rank, becoming aide-de-camp to Gen. Adna R. Chaffee, architect of the Army's prewar armored forces. General Chaffee stressed coordinated operations between air and ground forces. In 1941 Lee, then a major, became Chief of Corps Aviation, I Armored Corps.

General Lee spent the bulk of World War II in the United States organizing, training, and commanding tactical air forces. Shortly after the Normandy invasion on June 6, 1944, General Lee joined Ninth Air Force as its deputy director for operations. There he worked for Maj. Gen. Hoyt S. Vandenberg, commander of the Ninth Air Force, and helped direct the operational planning for the command's three thousand fighter, bomber, reconnaissance, and transport aircraft as it supported Lt. Gen. Omar N. Bradley's 12th Army Group in the advance across France into Germany.

General Lee's immediate postwar service focused on creating the Air Force's Tactical Air Command. He became the command's first chief of staff, its second deputy commander, and its second commander. Working with the first TAC commander, Major General "Pete" Quesada, and with Col. William W. Momyer, assistant chief of staff, Lee helped develop a comprehensive tactical air doctrine based on the experiences in World War II.   Codified to a degree in Air Force manuals, this tactical air doctrine was coordinated with the other services before the Korean War.   General Lee did not go to Korea; instead he spent the first part of the war in the

Pacific commanding a special air group which conducted hydrogen bomb tests on Eniwetok Island. In July 1951 he went to Headquarters USAF as the deputy director, then the director, of plans. After two years in Washington, he left for Europe as commander of the Twelfth Air Force, joining Gen. Lauris Norstad, CINCUSAFE (Commander in Chief, United States Air Forces in Europe). At that time the Twelfth Air Force was a joint command consisting of American, Canadian, and French air units, and it was the largest air force in the North Atlantic Treaty Organization (NATO). When Lee left Europe in 1957, he returned to the United States, assuming command of Ninth Air Force, Tactical Air Command.

In 1959 General Lee switched from offensive to defensive tactical air operations, serving successively as the vice commander and commander of the Air Defense Command. Four years later he took up his final assignment, air deputy to the Supreme Allied Commander, Europe. He retired from active duty in 1966.

William W. Momyer became an aviation cadet in the Army Air Corps in 1938. He graduated from basic pilot training and advanced pursuit schooling and received his commission at Kelly Field, Texas, in 1939. He began his career as a fighter pilot. Reassigned in February 1941, Momyer went to Cairo, Egypt, as an air observer and technical advisor to the British Royal Air Force (RAF). There he assisted in equipping RAF units with P–40 fighters. Returning to the States in the fall of 1941, Momyer helped organize and train fighter groups at Mitchel Field, New York, and Bolling Field, Washington, D.C. In October 1942 he led the 33d Fighter Group to Europe and participated in the North African campaign. He accumulated more than two hundred combat hours and eight confirmed aircraft kills while flying combat missions in the Tunisian, Sicilian, and Naples-Foggia campaigns.

In 1944 Momyer returned to the United States and became head of the panel evaluating combined air operations for the Army Air Forces Board. There he helped develop doctrines regarding air-to-ground combat operations. Immediately after World War II, he worked with Generals Quesada and Lee in establishing the Tactical Air Command. Beginning in 1949, Momyer spent five years in professional military schools, either as a student or a lecturer. Posted to Korea in August 1954, he began a series of command assignments: 8th Fighter-Bomber Wing (Korea), 314th Air Division (Korea), 312th Fighter-Bomber Wing (New Mexico), and 823d Air

Division (New Mexico). Reassigned to Langley Air Force Base (AFB) Virginia in 1958, General Momyer spent the next six years planning and defining new aircraft requirements, first at Headquarters TAC as director of plans and then at Headquarters USAF as director of operational requirements. In August 1964 he became commander of the Air Training Command.

With the buildup of US forces in Southeast Asia in the mid–1960s, General Momyer left the training arena for a combat command assignment in Saigon, South Vietnam. In July 1966 he became Gen. William C. Westmoreland's deputy commander for air operations and, simultaneously, commander of Seventh Air Force. In that war he was involved in a nearly continuous stream of close air support and interdiction operations, including Rolling Thunder, Tally Ho, Tiger Hound, and Niagara (Khe Sanh). In 1968 he returned to the United States as commander of TAC. Five years later, after witnessing the withdrawal of American forces from Southeast Asia and the inception of a new generation of fighters—the F–15 and F–16—General Momyer retired.

Lt. Gen. Elwood R. "Pete" Quesada ranks among the foremost leaders in the development of tactical air doctrine in the Air Force. Quesada enlisted in 1924 as a flying cadet in the Army Air Service, and from that moment his flying skills and personality placed him with that small band of air leaders— Spaatz, Eaker, Andrews, and Arnold—who created the U.S. Army Air Corps in World War II and the US Air Force in the postwar years. In 1929 Quesada was a crewmember with Spaatz and Eaker on the famed *Question Mark* aircraft which set a sustained inflight record, using air-to-air refueling, of 151 hours aloft. This flight established Quesada's reputation as a pilot, and throughout the 1930s he acted as the personal pilot for many national figures: F. Trubee Davison, Assistant Secretary of War for Air; Hugh S. Johnson, Administrator, National Recovery Administration; and Secretary of War George H. Dern. Between these flying assignments, he completed the Army Command and General Staff School at Fort Leavenworth, Kansas, and served as an air attaché to Cuba and Argentina, respectively. Upon his return from Argentina in late 1940, Quesada worked on the Air Corps staff as Arnold's foreign liaison chief. The following April he accompanied Arnold to London to arrange the details of lend-lease with British air leaders.

In July 1941 General Quesada, then a major, accepted command of the

33d Pursuit Group at Mitchel Field, New York. Eighteen months later, in December 1942, he was a brigadier general commanding the 1st Air Defense Wing as it prepared to go to North Africa. In Africa Quesada assumed command of the XII Fighter Command and quickly gained a reputation as a "pilot's general." Flying missions over Tunisia, Morocco, Sicily, Corsica, and southern Italy, General Quesada wrestled with many of the problems and issues discussed in this interview— distinctions between close air support and air superiority, difficulties in getting access to senior army commanders, and the inherent problems in trying to shift one's thinking from leading a squadron or group to commanding numerous flying units in continuous theater air operations. General Quesada acknowledged the debt that American air leaders owed to the British Royal Air Force in the North African campaign, citing specifically RAF Vice Air Marshal Sir Arthur Coningham as the seminal commander in developing the techniques for effective tactical air operations.

Late in the fall of 1943, General Quesada transferred to England and began preparations for the Allied invasion of France. Selected to command the IX Fighter Command, he began training and organizing its 36,000 people, 13 P–47 groups, 3 P–38 groups, and 2 P–51 groups (approximately 1,500 aircraft) for the Normandy invasion. When the invasion came Quesada set up his advanced headquarters for the expanded and redesignated IX Tactical Air Command on Omaha Beach on the first day after D–Day. Directing fighters and pursuit aircraft in close air support and interdiction missions, he and the IX Tactical Air Command supported Allied armies across France and into Germany in 1944 and 1945.

Following the war, Major General Quesada held varied leadership roles in intelligence and tactical air forces, becoming the first commander of Tactical Air Command (March 1946 to November 1948). He then turned his efforts to several special planning projects for the newly created Joint Chiefs of Staff. In October 1951 he retired from active duty and entered business in Washington, D.C. When Congress created the Federal Aviation Agency in August 1958, President Dwight D. Eisenhower chose Lt. Gen. Pete Quesada as the agency's first administrator. Four years later he "retired" again.

Air superiority concepts changed over time. In World War I the idea of air superiority was to win and maintain complete control over the airspace through the destruction of the enemy's air forces. Experience proved that

Not as much thought was given to air superiority in early years of aviation as to developing aircraft as tools of war. Among the imaginative and courageous ventures in experimentation was inflight refueling. In January 1929, the "Question Mark" set a 7-day world endurance record in such an experiment. In this venture, Lt. Elwood R. Quesada (top), member of the team, adjusts a gas line. (Bottom) The crew of this aircraft included: (l. to r.) Sgt. Roy Hooe, Lt. Elwood R. Quesada, Lt. Harry Halverson, Capt. Ira C. Eaker, and Maj. Carl A. Spaatz.

this idea was impractical and seldom, if ever, achievable. So the concept evolved in World War II into theater counter-air force operations. The practice was to carry out continuous and intensive operations in a limited area to gain and maintain as much air superiority and provide as much security from hostile air operations as possible.

This statement, clear today, was not well defined before World War II. Then American air leaders were occupied with developing strategic bombing concepts and did not develop doctrine for tactical air force operations. The air combat experiences of World War I, learned under the leadership of Brig. Gen. William "Billy" Mitchell, were never assimilated into tactical air training and planning in the interwar years. Instead individual pilots, such as Capt. Claire L. Chennault, Capt. Ralph F. Stearley, and Maj. John M. "Polo" Clark, seemed to have developed air tactics in the 1930s on their own initiative. This situation changed somewhat in the years between 1939 and 1941 as the European war began with Germany's invasion and conquest of Poland, Belgium, Denmark, France, and the Scandinavian nations. Suddenly American airmen were thrust into roles as air observers of large-scale air battles, such as the Battle of Britain in July–November 1940. At the same time Army Air Corps leaders were directing air forces in very large Army maneuvers in the United States. Neither of these two experiences, observing or exercising, was an adequate substitute for wartime experiences.[1]

Air superiority as an idea reached full maturity during World War II. In the American experience, air superiority over enemy forces was tested first in North Africa. There, as Generals Momyer and Quesada recall vividly, British Royal Air Force leaders showed the way in asserting the primacy of air superiority and centralized control over all theater air operations by an air commander. According to RAF Air Vice Marshal Arthur Coningham, the principal air leader in western Africa, air superiority had to be achieved before close air support and interdiction missions could be carried out. Without air superiority the other tactical air missions would be inconsequential. In January 1943 British Field Marshal Bernard L. Montgomery issued a small pamphlet, "Some Notes on High Command

---

[1]To read further on the difficult and complex times faced by air leaders from 1919 to 1939, see Dewitt S. Copp, *A Few Great Captains: The Men and Events that Shaped the Development of U.S. Air Power* (Garden City, N.Y., 1980); Robert T. Finney, *History of the Air Corps Tactical School, 1920–1940* (USAF Hist Study 100, Maxwell AFB, Ala., 1955); John F. Shiner, *Foulois and the U.S. Army Air Corps, 1931–1935* (Washington, 1982); Thomas H. Greer, *The Development of Air Doctrine in the Army Air Arm, 1917–1941* (USAF Hist Study 89, Maxwell AFB, Ala., 1955).

in War," in which he emphasized that the greatest asset of air power in war was its flexibility. "Nothing could be more fatal to the successful results," he declared, "than to dissipate the air resources into small packets placed under command of army formation commanders." All air resources had to be controlled, Montgomery asserted, by an air officer.[2]

In the United States Gen. George C. Marshall, Army chief of staff, agreed with Montgomery. To American air leaders who had long cherished an independent air force, Montgomery's pronouncement based on combat experience seemed prophetic. Within six months leaders of the Army Air Forces had set up a board, revised official tactical air doctrine, and issued new doctrine: War Department Field Manual 100–20, *Command and Employment of Air Power* dated July 21, 1943. This manual, stating categorically the primacy of air superiority for tactical air forces, has been added as an appendix to this interview.

What had been achieved in North Africa was verified by combat in Western Europe in 1944–45. In June 1944 the Allies invaded Normandy, France, and tactical air forces achieved air superiority, provided close air support to the ground armies, and flew interdiction missions to keep the enemy forces and supplies off the battlefield. Prior to the Normandy invasion serious, sustained arguments developed among British and American air leaders on the proper use of air power. These arguments turned less on the issue of establishing Allied air superiority over the German Air Force than on the role of Allied strategic air forces in a preinvasion interdiction bombing campaign. In late March 1944 Gen. Dwight D. Eisenhower, commander of the Allied Expeditionary Force, decided the issue with a personal directive stating:

> The first prerequisite of success in the maintenance of the combined bomber offensive and of our re-entry on the Continent is an overall reduction of the enemy's air combat strength and particularly his air fighter strength. The primary role of our air

[2]Years later Montgomery revealed how much he learned about air power. "When I myself rose to high command in 1942, I laid it down as an axiom that you must win the air battle before embarking on the land or sea battle. But as the war progressed and my experience grew, I decided that was not quite right: it was necessary to gain, as far as possible, 'mastery in the air' over the area of operations—and that principle saw me through to the end of the war." Nor did Montgomery doubt air power's value: "As airpower grew and developed, it was able to prevent movement in daylight to any appreciable degree, so much so that it became necessary to gain mastery in the air before beginning a land battle." [Montgomery of Alamein, Bernard L. Montgomery, *A History of Warfare* (Cleveland, 1968), pp 504,15.]

forces in the European and Mediterranean theaters is, therefore, to secure and maintain air superiority.[3]

In the Korean War air superiority as a tactical doctrine was never questioned explicitly. Instead, the issue arose indirectly in the form of questioning centralized command and control over tactical air forces. Army, Marine, and Navy commanders all differed in their understanding of the organization of tactical air support. At the beginning of the war, air support for ground forces could be readily furnished since American air forces had destroyed North Korea's small air force (120 aircraft) in the first few weeks of combat. Paradoxically, this achievement did not lessen demands on air power as requirements for close air support and interdiction missions increased when United Nations land and naval forces mounted counterattacks against the North Koreans. Some ground commanders leading special attack forces, such as at the Inchon amphibious landings near Seoul, Korea, wanted operational command and control over all forces, including air. At first General of the Army Douglas MacArthur, Commander in Chief, United Nations Command/Far East Command, authorized their requests. Almost immediately Lt. Gen. George E. Stratemeyer, Commander, Far East Air Forces, countered that as air commander he had to have centralized control of all air forces in the theater if they were to be used effectively. MacArthur agreed, although the dispute over the precise meaning of centralized and operational control festered between the services for much of the war. The dispute was not insubstantial. In the end, neither the Navy, Marines nor Army accepted the Air Force's position. Each developed alternate interpretations about command and control, coordination, and centralization of command over tactical air forces.

In Korea, Air Force arguments for centralized control were unquestionably bound up with the status of the service as an independent, coequal, military department. But they also concerned the belief by tactical air leaders that they had to respond to tactical requirements quickly and

---

[3]For a discussion of Eisenhower's decision see W. W. Rostow, *Pre-Invasion Bombing Strategy: General Eisenhower's Decision of 25 March 1944* (Austin, Tex., 1981). A basic resource for all aspects of American air operations in the war is Wesley F. Craven and James L. Cate, eds, *The Army Air Forces in World War II*, 7 vols (Chicago, 1948–58). Charles K. Webster and Noble Frankland's *The Strategic Air Offensive Against Germany, 1939–1945*, 4 vols (London, 1961), details the strategy, tactics, technology, and logistics of the Royal Air Force Bomber Command's campaigns. More specialized works that concentrate on the tactical air forces are Denis Richards and Hilary St. George Saunders, *Royal Air Force, 1939–1945*, 3 vols (London, 1953–54), and Kenn C. Rust, *The 9th Air Force in World War II* (Fallbrook, Calif., 1967).

decisively. This latter point became significant in 1951–52 when the Chinese Communist Air Force, equipped with Mig–15s, contested the airspace over North Korea. In order to mount an appropriate response, American F–86 Sabre jets had to be concentrated and redirected into missions that would maintain the "accustomed" air superiority achieved earlier in the war. American jets won that series of air battles so decisively that, as General Momyer stated in this interview, "In the Korean war there wasn't a single attack that I have been able to identify that was put against our ground forces." This observation, according to General Momyer, held for the war in Southeast Asia as well: "Our Army and Navy enjoyed complete immunity from attacks by the North Vietnamese Air Force. Our deployments of troops, locations of supply points, and concentrations of ships in ports were never restrained because of a threat from the North Vietnamese Air Force."[4]

Whether one explains this situation by the peculiarity of wars waged in Korea and Southeast Asia, attributes it to superior over inferior aeronautical technology, or interprets it as the product of better training, one thing remains clear: air leaders should not ignore the need for air superiority in future wars and the changing nature of the challenges to gaining unfettered use of airspace.[5]

Several individuals contributed to producing this Project Warrior study. The questions were first developed by the Oral History Division, Albert F. Simpson Historical Research Center: Lt. Col. Arthur W. McCants, Jr., Dr. James C. Hasdorff, Mr. Hugh N. Ahmann, and Capt. Mark C. Cleary. Colonel McCants, Mr. Ahmann, and Captain Cleary recorded the interview and oversaw the initial typing and editing. Col. John Schlight, Deputy Chief, Office of Air Force History, edited the questions into a coherent whole. While several historians and officers suggested participants for the interview, Col. Schlight made the final recommendations and from the beginning managed the interview for the Office of Air Force History. Reference specialists, Mr. William C. Heimdahl, Capt. Susan Cober, and SMSgt Alden R. Hargett of the Office of Air Force

---

[4]Gen William W. Momyer, USAF, Ret, *Air Power in Three Wars (WW II, Korea, Vietnam)* (Washington, 1978), pp 158–59.

[5]For those interested in reading further on the use of airpower in Korea, three books are recommended: Robert F. Futrell, *The United States Air Force in Korea, 1950–1953* (New York, 1961); James A. Field, Jr., *History of United States Naval Operations: Korea* (Washington, 1962); and Momyer, *Air Power in Three Wars (WW II, Korea, Vietnam)*.

History, and Mrs. Pat Tugwell and Mr. Lyle Minter, Army Library in the Pentagon, assisted in the research for the footnotes and introductory essay. In the Office of Air Force History, four editors—Mr. Lawrence J. Paszek, Mr. Eugene P. Sagstetter, Mrs. Anne E. Shermer, and Ms. Bobbi Levien— assisted in the preparation and layout of the final manuscript. Mr. Renan Del Villar of Air Force Publishing Division designed the graphics.

Air Superiority in World War II and Korea

Participants	Active Duty Years
Gen. James Ferguson, USAF, Retired	1934–70
Gen. Robert M. Lee, USAF, Retired	1931–66
Gen. William W. Momyer, USAF, Retired	1938–73
Lt. Gen. Elwood R. Quesada, USAF, Retired	1924–51
Dr. Richard H. Kohn, Chief, Office of Air Force History	

Kohn:　Let me welcome you on behalf of the Air Force and thank you for taking a morning out of your busy schedules to share your experiences with us. The Historical Program selected air superiority as the topic for discussion because it seemed to us to be as vital today as it has been in the past. Air superiority is a primary mission for the Air Force; it is perhaps the single most important prerequisite for all other forms of air warfare and the exploitation of the air environment in warfare. We suspect that in recent times air superiority has been neglected in the spectrum of competing ideas and thinking on strategy, tactics, and air doctrine.

　　We hope to keep this interview, as much as possible, focused on the years before 1955. We believe the present needs to be informed by the past. As historians we believe the past is the most crucial guide to the future. And we fear that some of those in the present are too confident; perhaps they have not heard enough, or know enough, about the past.

Momyer:　I think it's going to be a little bit difficult to cast it completely within the limitations of 1955. I think you are going to have to range a little bit beyond 1955, it seems to me, if you are going to draw on some of the current experience, without getting in and fighting the Vietnam War per se. But if you are really going to raise some of the fundamental questions about how important air superiority is, and what the meaning of air superiority is, then I think you are going to have to go back and forth in your illustrations. I

13

would suggest that we not necessarily constrict ourselves just to pre 1955 per se.

Kohn: Can we focus it there, General Momyer?

Momyer: I would say start out on the pre-World War II era, particularly with General Quesada and General Lee, as kind of a kickoff to then start drawing on their experiences, particularly in World War II.

Kohn: I think that would be fine.

The Pre-World War II Era

Kohn: Let me begin by asking whether before World War II we thought much about air superiority. The belief in the Air Corps Tactical School[1] was that the airplane could reach the economic and political heart of a nation, thereby defeating that nation, leaping over opposing armies and navies. How was this thought to be possible? How widely was that thinking held? Was there a lack of attention to the question of air superiority, and did that inattention prove difficult once the war began?

Quesada: Well, I will start out, mainly because I am the oldest guy here and was in a remote way involved in that psychology. As you suggest, there was a definite school of thought within what was then the Air Service that they could, with immunity, assert a strategic influence on a conflict. There was almost an ignorant disregard of the requirement of air superiority. It was generally felt, without a hell of a lot of thought being given to it, that if there should occur an air combat, or a defense against the ability to

---

[1]This school had been established as the Air Service Field Officers School in October 1920 at Langley Field, Virginia. In November 1922 the school's name was changed to the Air Service Tactical School. In 1926, when the Air Service became the Air Corps, the school became known as the Air Corps Tactical School. In July 1931 it moved from Langley to Maxwell Field, Alabama, and was active through the decade of the thirties. The instructors and students at the school developed air doctrine. In 1940 the school closed. With the advent of World War II, however, a similar school, teaching air doctrine and operational tactics, opened at Orlando, Florida. [Robert T. Finney, *History of the Air Corps Tactical School, 1920–1940* (USAF Hist Study 100, Maxwell AFB, Ala., 1955).] Two general guides to the history of air power in books and articles are Samuel D. Miller's *An Aerospace Bibliography* (Washington, 1978) and Robin Higham's *Air Power: A Concise History* (New York, 1972).

envelop, it would occur at the target. That was the thinking of the time. It might interest you to know who the architects of this thinking were. When I cite them, I do it with a compliment to them; because, where they might have been a little bit wrong in detail, they were in fact very imaginative and very courageous. Of course, everybody knows that Billy Mitchell[2] was a factor in it, but he wasn't *the* one who molded air force opinion of the time. People who molded that opinion of the time were basically "Tooey" Spaatz,[3] Gen. Frank Andrews,[4] and Gen. George Kenney.[5] A fellow named Ennis Whitehead[6] was also very active in this. In that group it was almost a fetish. They molded the thinking of enveloping. I don't mean to be critical, but history has to be remembered and written within the context of its time: what was happening then. There was practically no consideration given to air superiority per se. That came along, I would imagine, around 1937

---

[2]Brig. Gen. William Mitchell (1879–1936). For a biography of Mitchell's tumultuous career as an advocate of air power, see Alfred F. Hurley, *Billy Mitchell: Crusader for Air Power,* 2d ed (Bloomington, Ind., 1975).

[3]Gen. Carl Spaatz (1891–1974). Among his assignments in World War II, Spaatz led the Eighth Air Force in Europe and served as commander of the U.S. Strategic Air Forces in Europe. In February 1946, following the retirement of Gen. Henry H. Arnold, he became Commanding General, Army Air Forces. In 1947 President Harry S. Truman appointed General Spaatz as the first Chief of Staff, United States Air Force. For a brief account of Spaatz's wartime leadership, see Alfred Goldberg, "Spaatz," in *The War Lords: Military Commanders of the Twentieth Century,* ed: Field Marshal Sir Michael Carver (Boston, 1976), pp 568–581. To gain a perspective on all Army Air Forces operations and activities in World War II, consult Wesley F. Craven and James L. Cate, eds, *The Army Air Forces in World War II,* 7 vols (Chicago, 1948–58).

[4]Lt. Gen. Frank M. Andrews (1884–1943). As a major general, he headed General Headquarters Air Force from 1935 to 1939. Subsequently demoted and exiled from this position for his advocacy of an independent modern air force, he was rescued in July 1939 by Gen. George C. Marshall, Deputy Chief of Staff, United States Army. Andrews served in Washington, D.C., as G–3, Assistant Chief of Staff for Operations and Training, until 1940. Then a lieutenant general, he went to the Caribbean, North Africa, and finally to Europe as commander of the U.S. Forces in the European Theater in late 1942. In May 1943, while on an inspection trip from England, his B–24 Liberator flew into a hill in Iceland during a driving snowstorm, killing all aboard. See DeWitt S. Copp, *Forged in Fire: Strategy and Decisions in the Airwar over Europe, 1940–45* (New York, 1982), pp ix–xii, 393–95; DeWitt S. Copp, *A Few Great Captains: The Men and Events that Shaped the Development of U.S. Air Power* (Garden City, N.Y., 1980).

[5]Gen. George C. Kenney (1889–1977). During World War I, Kenney saw combat and rose to the rank of captain in the Army Air Service. In the interwar years he developed innovations in equipment and tactics, and he worked to achieve an independent air force. In World War II he became Gen. Douglas MacArthur's commander of the Allied Air Forces in the Southwest Pacific. Following the war, he commanded the Strategic Air Command (1946–48) and Air University (1948–51). The best account of his leadership of the southwest Pacific air forces in World War II is George C. Kenney, *General Kenney Reports: A Personal History of the Pacific War* (New York, 1949).

[6]Lt. Gen. Ennis C. Whitehead (1895–1964). A fighter pilot in World War I, Whitehead served in the Army Air Corps in the decades between the two world wars. In World War II he commanded the Fifth Air Force in the southwest Pacific theater. After the war, he was commander of the Far East Air Forces (1945–49). For Whitehead's World War II experiences, see George C. Kenney, *General Kenny Reports: A Personal History of the Pacific War (New York, 1949).*

when air superiority began to creep into the thinking. What was then called the pursuit airplane was generally, as I remember it, considered a defensive weapon that would remain static until called into play to fight. It wasn't until 1937 and later on that we began to recognize that the enemy would adopt the philosophy that we ourselves had adopted: that is, they would defend. It wasn't until early World War II that we really began to give serious consideration to the fact that, in order for the strategic effort to be effective, we had to be able to cope with fighting opposing defensive forces over our target. World War II brought that about.

Momyer: How is it, in your judgment, that we lost our air superiority experience from World War I? Look at the dogfights. Dogfights were essentially nothing but combat for control of the air, whether you call it air superiority or not. It came out in World War I, theoretically, with the pursuit airplane. The pursuit airplane was primarily to fight other pursuit airplanes, to shoot down balloons, and to shoot down any kind of reconnaissance activity. There is a gap, it just seems to me as I have looked back through the history, a complete gap, until you get probably almost to the time of Chennault.[7] I don't think it is really clear—maybe you can amplify that—what Chennault's concept was of pursuit aviation. If you will look in all the readings about what he said, he kept talking about air defense or defense of the United States in terms of pursuit and talked about bombardment escort. Can you amplify what you think Chennault thought about air superiority at that time?

Quesada: If I had expanded my remarks and thought of Chennault, which I would not have—you reminded me of it—I would have to say that he made a big impact on this problem. Don't forget that before we were in the war he was on the battleline fighting. He learned through experience that in order for your enveloping force to be effective you had to do something about its air defense. Whether he thought of it as creating a situation over our targets that gave us superiority of the air, I just don't

---

[7]Maj. Gen. Claire L. Chennault (1890–1958). Though he served in World War I, Chennault did not get his pilot's wings until 1919. Thereafter he became an advocate of pursuit aviation. Chennault taught and did some writing while at the Air Corps Tactical School in the 1930s, publishing in 1933 *The Role of Defensive Pursuit* which served as a student text for many years. In 1937 Chennault retired from the Army Air Corps and soon went to China. There, he began organizing the famous Flying Tiger squadrons. See Maj. Gen. Claire L. Chennault, USAF, Ret., *Way of a Fighter: The Memoirs of Claire Lee Chennault* (New York, 1949), and Bernard Nalty, *Tigers Over Asia* (New York, 1978).

know. Chennault was the great advocate of pursuit aviation. He carried the ball, and almost boringly so. He was a pain in the ass to a lot of people. He did turn out to be quite right, as many people who are pains in the ass do.

Momyer: Almost in that same pre-world war time period, we had the Spanish Civil War, with the German Condor Legion, and the forces of the Soviet Union.[8] You had really a semistrategic bombing campaign, for example, with the bombing of Madrid and the escort and the fighter engagements that took place there. Yet, looking back, I can't find much interpretation of that. I can't find much codification. I guess what I am really coming to is that up to World War II, I can't find much codification of what we really thought about how we would employ air, except for the strategic forces. You had strategic thinking, of course, with AWPD–1—the war plan—as you well know, for the targeting of Germany.[9] But I guess a theory of air superiority in terms of its relationship to the ground forces was totally missing.

Quesada: Well, "Spike" [General Momyer], I was trying to say, with-

---

[8]In July 1936 the Spanish government was challenged by an armed insurrection led by Gen. Francisco Franco. A series of incidents developed quickly into a civil war of international consequences. In September 1936 Joseph Stalin sent Russian bombers and tanks to Spain, and they joined with the Spanish government forces. The day after the first engagement, employing Soviet forces, Adolf Hitler directed the German Condor legion—a small elite air unit of about one hundred dive bombers, fighters, reconnaissance planes, and experimental aircraft to fly to Spain and join forces with General Franco and the nationalist forces. A short time later, Benito Mussolini dispatched Italian air and naval forces to Spain in support of the nationalists. Throughout the Spanish Civil War (1936–39), many cities (Barcelona, Zaragoza, Guernica, and Madrid) were repeatedly attacked from the air. The destruction of urban centers, for nearly three centuries largely removed from most of the ravages of war, was cited by supporters of strategic bombing as evidence for the validity of their concepts. See Hugh Thomas, *The Spanish Civil War*, rev ed (New York, 1977), pp 468–484.

[9]AWPD–1 was the fundamental American plan for waging the European air war during World War II. The plan specified that the Army Air Forces would need 257 air groups equipped with 61,799 operational combat aircraft and 37,051 training aircraft. This force would be manned by 179,398 officers and 1,939,337 enlisted men. Written quickly in August 1941, the plan focused on production of quotas and training schedules for the men slated to fly and maintain the wartime air force. Air planners in 1941 operated from two assumptions: construction of an interim air force based on airplanes then in production or in advanced production; and designing and building a strategic air force centered around a new generation of long-range bombers. See Haywood S. Hansell, Jr., *The Air Plan That Defeated Hitler* (Atlanta, Ga., 1972); Wesley F. Craven and James L. Cate, eds, *The Army Air Forces in World War II*, 7 vols (Chicago, 1948-58), Vol I: *Plans and Early Operations, January 1939 to August 1942*, 131–32, 146–159; Maurice Matloff and Edwin M. Snell, *Strategic Planning for Coalition Warfare, 1941–1942* [U.S. Army in World War II, The War Department], (Washington, 1953), pp 59–60; Irving B. Holley, Jr., *Buying Aircraft: Materiel Procurement for the Army Air Forces* [U.S. Army in World War II, Special Studies], (Washington, 1964), pp 155–58, 166–68; Alfred Goldberg, ed, *A History of the United States Air Force, 1907–1957* (Princeton, N.J., 1957), pp 47–55.

out knowing it, what you have recited. I think during that period, we really didn't know what we were trying to do. We were doing it but not defining it. Air superiority, or the concept of air superiority was, in my opinion, really defined after the second World War started. In Spain it was used in a sort of half-assed way, but I don't think it was defined. Let me go back to your comment about World War I. When you look back—really as we think now—the fighter airplane in those days was basically an ego trip. The fighter airplane didn't do a hell of a lot of good. They would go up and fight each other and create aces, but there was no great strategic effort that was being executed or fulfilled. Basically—I don't mean it in an unattractive way—the fighter business in those days was a bunch of guys going up and fighting another bunch of guys without a known objective.

Momyer: I think our preoccupation with the strategic concept of war did more to frustrate any thinking on the employment of other aspects of aviation. If you will look at our pre-World War II writing, it's almost all devoted to the employment of strategic aviation against the heartland of a nation. If one were able to overfly enemy ground forces, overfly his naval forces, and get at the source of his power, one could bring the war to a conclusion without defeating his military forces.

Robert M. Lee, Jr.,
as a first lieutenant.

P-26 pursuit aircraft, flown in three-ship formation.

Lee: I came in a little later than Pete [General Quesada]. But I would like to speak from the viewpoint of a second lieutenant, a wingman, in the 20th Pursuit Group in about the 1932–33–34 period when we had P–12s and P–26s. It's true that air superiority per se was not much considered. My group commander was "Miff" Harmon.[10] He had a couple of good squadron commanders, three of them: "Pete" Pearcy, John "Polo" Clark, and Clarence Crumrine. Now Polo Clark was, I think, the greatest thinker among these. The fact of the matter was that, when he had the 77th Pursuit Squadron, he developed the two-ship formation; everybody else was flying three-ship formations at that time. He insisted on his squadron flying the

---

[10]Lt. Gen. Millard F. Harmon (1888–1946). From October 1932 to October 1936, Harmon led the 20th Pursuit Group, based at Barksdale Field, Louisiana. The three squadrons in the group were commanded by Capt. Charles G. Pearcy, Maj. John M. Clark, and Capt. Clarence E. Crumrine.

Formation of B-3 bomber aircraft over Long Beach, California, during the 1933 March
Field maneuvers.

two-ship formation with the wingman covering the leader. I think he was the man who started that.

Our mission in pursuit at that time was air patrol and searching for bombers. As was mentioned, there was some thought of protection of some sort, either air defense or protection of the bombers. If we were escorting bombers, which we did in the 1933 maneuvers out at March Field [California], we would fly high cover up there for them.[11] On the other hand, our exercises in the Barksdale Field [Louisiana]–Galveston [Texas] area—the 3d Attack Group was at Fort Crockett, Texas—the philosophy at that time, as we understood, was for the attack squadrons to come in at low level with their A–3s, A–12s, or whatever they might have, and we would fly patrol searching for them. We would be spread out. We might have some intelligence of a possible target they were going to hit, but we didn't know the direction; therefore, you would fly a rather widely separated patrol. When somebody saw the attackers, you would holler "Tallyho" and start for them. I think there was a certain amount of emphasis watching for hostile pursuit planes. Both Claire Chennault and Ennis Whitehead came to our group. We did a few hours each month of "individual aerial combat." Ennis Whitehead, I believe, came first and then Chennault a little later. Ennis Whitehead became group operations officer in 1933 or 1934, and Chennault a little later, about 1935. I think about then they started thinking a little bit more about keeping the air clear of enemy airplanes. However, they didn't think in terms of bombing airfields too much, as I remember it. Is that right, Pete?

Quesada: You are absolutely right. It was almost an unheard of concept in that time period.

Lee: A little later than the period you are talking about—Spike was mentioning that air superiority developed during World War II. I think the implementation took place then; however, I happened to be on a committee

---

[11]Approximately three hundred airplanes participated in the three-week exercise held at March Field, California, from May 8 to 29, 1933. The exercises were under the command of Brig. Gen. Oscar Westover and tested concepts of bombing, pursuit, reconnaissance, and close air support. Eight years later the Army staged massive maneuvers in Texas and Louisiana in August and September 1941. These maneuvers involved more than four hundred thousand troops, armored tanks, paratroopers, and more than a thousand aircraft, and were important for the testing of training concepts and combat doctrine and for the selection and promotion of Army commanders. See Forrest C. Pogue, *George C. Marshall: Ordeal and Hope, 1939–1942* (New York, 1966), pp 162–65.

right at the beginning of the war when Ralph Stearley,[12] who had been an instructor at the tactical school in attack aviation, was called by General Arnold[13] to write a manual. I think it was called 100–20, wasn't it? One of the first manuals which was—no, that was a different one. That was support of ground forces. This one he and his committee wrote was one on the use of air power. I recall then that in the manual one of the first prerequisites to proper use of land and air forces was "air superiority." The word air superiority developed in that manual. Do you remember that manual?

Quesada: I don't remember, but that was a period—the first period I can recall—when it was even brought up.

Lee: I would say the beginning of 1940, right along in there sometime.

Quesada: That's right. World War II.

Momyer: Did you see any of that, though, in the pre-World War II maneuvers?

---

[12]Maj. Gen. Ralph F. Stearley (1898–1973). From 1936 to 1940 Stearley was at the Air Corps Tactical School. During World War II, he held a variety of AAF posts, including command of state-side tactical units. In June 1943 Colonel Stearley, Col. Morton H. McKinnon, AAF, and Lt. Col. Orin H. Moore, USA, wrote War Department Field Manual 100–20, *Command and Employment of Air Power*. The manual was published on July 21, 1943, and became the fundamental doctrinal statement of operational independence for the Army Air Forces. It was also a major step toward an independent Air Force, established in September 1947. (The manual is reprinted as an appendix to this volume.)

[13]Gen. Henry H. Arnold (1886–1950). Graduated from West Point in 1908, Arnold subsequently became identified in his life and career with the development of military aeronautics in the United States. The Wright brothers taught Arnold to fly in 1911, and in the years before World War I he set numerous aeronautical records. During World War I, Arnold reached the rank of temporary colonel, serving in the Office of the Director of Military Aeronautics, War Department General Staff. In the interwar years Arnold, reduced in rank to major, remained in the Army Air Corps and worked to further military aviation. In 1925 he testified in support of Brig. Gen. Billy Mitchell, then on trial at a court-martial for insubordination for advocating an independent Air Force. During the 1930s, Arnold organized and led a flight of ten Martin B–10 bombers on the famed round-trip flight to Alaska from Washington, D.C. Subsequently, he was placed in command of the 1st Wing, General Headquarters Air Force, March Field, California, and was instrumental in encouraging the development of both the B–17 and B–24 bombers before World War II. In late September 1938, Arnold became Chief of the Air Corps, United States Army, with the rank of major general. During World War II, General Arnold directed all U.S. air forces against Germany and Japan. The Army Air Forces expanded during the war from 22,000 officers and men and 3,900 airplanes to 2,500,000 men and 75,000 aircraft. During the war, General Arnold suffered several heart attacks and after the war he was succeeded by Gen. Carl Spaatz in February 1946. Arnold died in January 1950. A recent popular biography is Thomas M. Coffey, *HAP: The Story of the U.S. Air Force and the Man Whou Built It, General Henry H. "Hap" Arnold.*(New York, 1982). Also recommended is John W. Huston, "The Wartime Leadership of 'Hap' Arnold," *Air Power and Warfare,* Proceedings of the 8th Military History Symposium, United States Air Force Academy, October 18–20, 1978 (Washington, 1979), pp 168–185.

Aviation Cadet
James Ferguson.

Lee: No.

Momyer: Could you see it in the Carolina maneuvers, Jim? You were down in the Carolinas.[14]

Ferguson: Yes, based on early reports from U.S. pilots participating with the RAF in Europe and by visits to these maneuvers by RAF Battle of Britain aces like Group Captain "Teddy" Donaldson, we gained some very helpful ideas on modern use of fighters.[15] Spike, we conducted "dawn patrols," as in World War I, along the Pee Dee River [North Carolina]. We also escorted light bombers to their targets and, in doing so, encountered "enemy air" which resulted in mock air combat.

---

[14]Army maneuvers in the Carolinas began on November 1, 1941, and terminated on December 5, 1941. These exercises involved the I and IV Armored Corps and tested tactical air-ground coordination and air defenses along the Atlantic coast from Massachusetts to North Carolina. See Forrest C. Pogue, *George C. Marshall: Ordeal and Hope, 1939–1942* (New York, 1966), pp 164–65.

[15]In the summer of 1941, RAF Wing Commander Edward M. "Teddy" Donaldson came to the United States and visited the U.S. Army Air Corps gunnery schools. Donaldson and other RAF officers

Northrop A-17s (like the one above) and Martin B-10s (on adjacent page)
were employed in simulated attacks during maneuvers.

Lee: I was in those maneuvers and the Louisiana maneuvers, too, then. It was like when Patton said to his invasion troops, "I have to tell my children that the first part of the war I was down in Louisiana shoveling s———."[16]

Quesada: I don't recall during that period—but I am not contradicting anybody because everybody's memory is better than mine now—that the concept of air superiority arose during those maneuvers. I recall a concept of envelopment arising, but I don't recall trying to bring out, and bring up, the defensive forces of the enemy. I just don't recall it. That doesn't mean it didn't happen.

Ferguson: Looking back to the Carolina maneuvers, and that was over

gave advice on fixed-gunnery methods, syllabi for courses, and some direct training. They also assisted the Army Air Forces in developing an integrated air-ground air defense system based on the British combat experiences in the Battle of Britain, July–November 1940. See Wesley F. Craven and James L. Cate, eds, *The Army Air Forces in World War II,* 7 vols (Chicago, 1948–58), Vol VI: *Men and Planes,* 481.

[16]Lt. Gen. George S. Patton, Jr.'s remarks were but part of a longer exhortation to the troops that he gave on several occasions during World War II. For a recapitulation of this Patton speech, see Martin Blumenson, ed, *The Patton Papers,* 2 vols (Boston, 1972–74), II, 456–58.

William W. Momyer during pilot training.

forty years ago, one can say that the transition from World War I expressions and tactics was evolving. Fighter sweeps, escort of attack and bomber formations as well as air-to-air combat became the pattern of operations. One very popular and, I think, successful tactic was very early morning— first light as the Brits would say—attacks against enemy airfields.

Quesada: I might inject, I don't have any knowledge of the Carolina maneuvers because I wasn't there. So in that respect I have misspoken.

Momyer: Yes, I was on those maneuvers. I recall that we were sent out in formations to intercept incoming bombers. We were sent out on formations to engage other fighters. But the primary emphasis during that entire maneuver was really in support of the ground forces. These were the kinds of missions, just like you said. I can remember taking off on so-called dawn patrol on airfield defense in anticipation of a bomber attack coming in, and then fighters were sent out for intercept. But the primary emphasis was put on that close air support.

Ferguson: The Muroc Lake maneuvers in 1936 simulated a fighter defense of a metropolitan area—in this case Los Angeles and nearby parts. We, the fighters, were the defenders flying Boeing P–36s. The attacking forces were equipped with B–10 bombers and A–17 attack aircraft.[17] The bombers came in on the attack too high for us to reach them, and the attackers used terrain masking to surprise us on the ground. With no other means of warning, we were caught and treated to a good dose of tear gas which took weeks to shake out of our blankets. Looking back, this experience helped General Arnold and others in Washington to persuade the Army staff that higher performance aircraft were needed.[18]

---

[17]Lying just east of Los Angeles, California, Muroc Dry Lake bombing range was the site of maneuvers in May 1936. Army Air Corps flying units, about three hundred planes and three thousand men, flew bombing and pursuit missions against Los Angeles. Brig. Gen. Henry H. "Hap" Arnold declared the maneuvers successful, though he noted that west coast air defenses were weak. [DeWitt S. Copp, *A Few Great Captains: The Men and Events the Shaped the Development of U.S. Air Power* (Garden City, N.Y., 1980), pp 388–89.]

[18]After the Muroc Dry Lake maneuvers, virtually all of the Army Air Corps leaders concluded that slow, medium-range bombers would not be able to survive against high-speed pursuit aircraft. Maj. Gen. Frank M. Andrews led the fight in the War Department for a multiengine, high-performance bomber. See Copp, *A Few Great Captains,* pp 388–392.

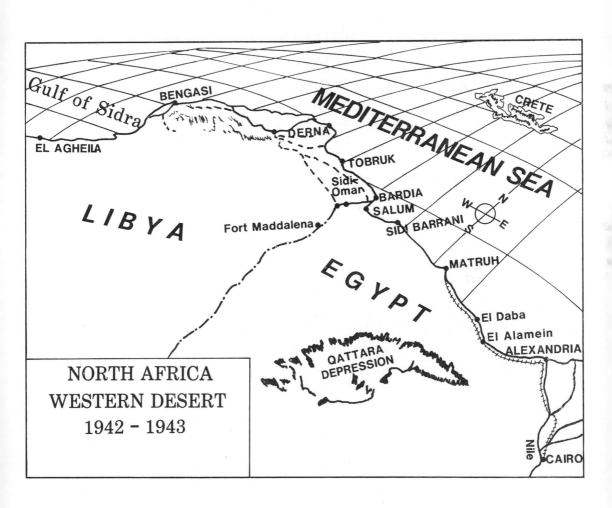

Gulf of Sidra

BENGASI

MEDITERRANEAN SEA

CRETE

DERNA

EL AGHEILA

TOBRUK

Sidi Oman

LIBYA

BARDIA

SALUM

Fort Maddalena

SIDI BARRANI

W — N — E — S

EGYPT

MATRUH

El Daba

El Alamein

ALEXANDRIA

QATTARA
DEPRESSION

Nile

CAIRO

NORTH AFRICA
WESTERN DESERT
1942 – 1943

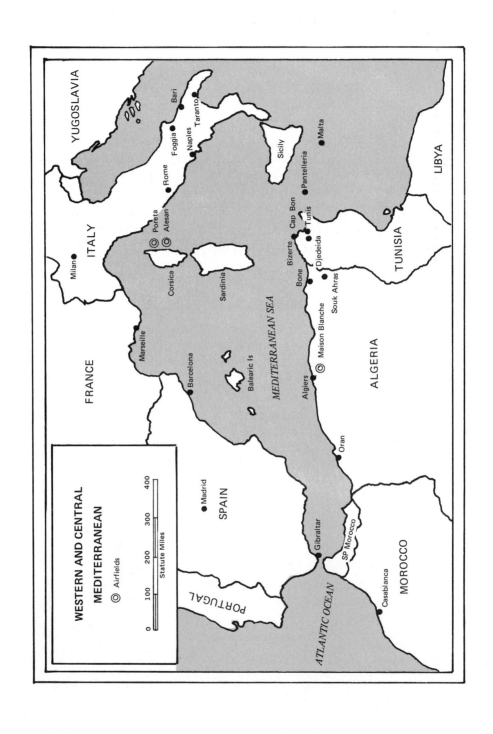

WESTERN AND CENTRAL
MEDITERRANEAN

◎ Airfields

Statute Miles

0   100   200   300   400

YUGOSLAVIA

Bari
Foggia
Taranto
Naples
Rome
Sicily
Malta

ITALY

Poreta
Alesan

Milan

Corsica

Sardinia

Pantelleria
Bizerte
Cap Bon
Tunis
Djedeida
Bone
Souk Ahras

TUNISIA

LIBYA

MEDITERRANEAN SEA

Marseille

Barcelona

Balearic Is

Algiers

◎ Maison Blanche

ALGERIA

FRANCE

Oran

Madrid

SPAIN

Gibraltar
SP Morocco
Casablanca

MOROCCO

PORTUGAL

ATLANTIC OCEAN

World War II

Kohn: While you have said that there wasn't a great deal of thought about air superiority and it wasn't really codified, what kinds of problems did this cause us as we went into World War II? How did you respond to what you found in the air war, once we were in the war? What lessons did you find as you looked in 1939, 1940, and 1941 at the fighting in Europe? Did we change our thinking? Did we learn anything in that period?

Momyer: I don't think there is any question about it. With the onset of the war—and General Quesada was intimately involved in this—we sent various teams—we had a team over in Europe, which Spaatz, if I remember correctly, headed up—to observe the operations that were going on there. I reported to him. At the time I was in a fighter group, and I was sent, under the cover of being an air attaché, out to the Western Desert.[19]

Quesada: And you have never forgiven me since.

Momyer: That's exactly right. I didn't get home until almost twelve months later. I was sent out to the Western Desert to take a look at what the British were doing. At that time Greece had been evacuated, and Crete had fallen, and the British had practically no airplanes at all in the Western Desert. From my observations, I think the British were really in the same kind of throes of developing their concept about what is rightly called now tactical air. I couldn't see any real hard and fast doctrine evolving. It seemed to me almost hit and miss. There were attacks against airfields, and that was becoming more systematic on the desert at the time. The interdiction attacks were definitely becoming more methodical with the severance of the sea lines of communication. You could see that pattern develop. I would say, of the doctrine that was coming out, there was less definitiveness in terms of close air support. People have looked at the RAF doctrine and some of the arguments that are going on today about close support. The

---

[19]Shortly after World War II began in Europe in September 1939, General Arnold sent Lt. Col. Carl A. Spaatz and Maj. George C. Kenney to Europe as combat observers. Remaining in Europe for several months, Spaatz and Kenney sent back detailed reports on the air war, reports that influenced Air Corps planners. When the Battle of Britain commenced in July 1940, several air officers were dispatched to England to observe the air battle. In April 1941 General Arnold went to England. See Wesley F. Craven and James L. Cate, eds, *The Army Air Forces in World War II*, 7 vols (Chicago, 1948–58), Vol VI: *Men and Planes*, 480–81.

British concept, as I could see it at that time, was not to use small numbers of aircraft for close support. When they went out to do it, they used large numbers, relatively large numbers. The maximum size force on the Western Desert at that time was about twelve hundred airplanes. When they did go out, aircraft were used like massed artillery. So I would say that those teams, at least the people on those teams, were very influential when they returned.

Some of the thinking of what air superiority meant was beginning to solidify. I don't want to monopolize—and Jim can pick it up here, and General Quesada—but when I went in on the North African invasion, I would say that, at that particular time, we really didn't have a definitive concept. When we deployed forward and our air got split up—the British were up on one part of the front, and we were on the other part of the front— it was becoming obvious that somebody was going to have to make decisions to go out and destroy the German air force in North Africa. That decision wasn't being made, because our air was so split up.

For example, my fighter group, which was the first in North Africa, was committed almost exclusively to flying what I call umbrella patrols over the frontline. In the meantime I can recall right today a German airfield at Kairouan, a German airfield at Sousse, a German airfield at Sfax, and about four others. From those German airfields they were consistently hitting our airfields. As a matter of fact, I was taking attacks three and four times a day, and yet there were no offensive actions going on against those German airfields. On the other hand, the strategic forces that were in North Africa at the time were bombing primarily ports. They were bombing some of the airfields in Sicily and some of the airfields over in Italy, but there was very little effort mounted against what I would call the tactical airfields. It wasn't really until the Casablanca conference of 1943 that this issue was really faced up to, or the fact that the air organization was really not suitable for the job that had to be done.[20] I know I am repeating a little bit of history,

---

[20]At the Casablanca conference held in Morocco in January 1943, President Franklin D. Roosevelt and Prime Minister Winston S. Churchill agreed to postpone plans for a direct invasion of Europe across the English Channel until late spring in 1944. In the interim the Allies would rely on a combined bomber offensive against Germany. In carrying out this policy, the British and American Combined Chiefs of Staff issued the "Casablanca Directive," spelling out the objectives of the bomber offensive from the United Kingdom against Germany. The Combined Chiefs of Staff also resolved certain organizational issues raised in Allied operations in North Africa. For air operations, the new organizational structure established an Allied air commander in chief, with two principal subordinates—an air commander for northwest Africa (Spaatz) and an air commander for the Middle East (Air Chief Marshal Sir Sholto Douglas). Spaatz's command included the Twelfth Air Force, Western Desert Air Force, and the Eastern Air Command.

At the Casablanca Conference, standing behind President Franklin D. Roosevelt and Prime Minister Winston Churchill are: (l. to r.) Gen. Henry H. ("Hap") Arnold, Adm. Ernest J. King, Gen. George C. Marshall, Adm. Sir Dudley Pound, Gen. Sir Alan Brooke, and Air Marshall Sir Charles Portal.

but the man who I felt really brought the thing together was Air Marshal Arthur Coningham.[21] "Maori" Coningham was probably the most knowledgeable British officer on tactical air operations, as a result of his experience on the Western Desert.

The Casablanca conference decided to establish the North African theater and the air components under it, in which the tactical air force was created, the Allied tactical air force [Northwest African Tactical Air Force]. At that time it brought together the XII Air Support Command, which had

---

[21]RAF Air Marshal Sir Arthur Coningham (1895–1948). As an Air Vice Marshal, he led the Royal Air Force in the Western Desert theater of North Africa. A native New Zealander, Coningham was given the nickname of "Maori" and it evolved through colloquial usage to become "Mary" to friends and associates. Working with Gen. Bernard L. Montgomery, he was instrumental in asserting the necessity for air superiority as a prerequisite for all other types of air operations. [Lord Arthur Tedder, *With Prejudice: The War Memoirs of a Marshal of the Royal Air Force* (Boston, 1966), pp 218–19; R. J. Overy, *The Air War, 1939–1945* (New York, 1981), pp 84–89; Sir Arthur Coningham, "The Development of Tactical Air Forces," *Journal of United Services Institute* IX (1946), 211–227; Shelford Bidwell and Dominick Graham, *Fire Power: British Army Weapons and Theories of War, 1904–1945* (Boston, 1982)].

almost exclusively been under II Corps.[22] If you wonder why some of us older people feel so strongly about our relationships to the Army, the XII Air Support Command, for all practical purposes, was under II Corps. At the time, II Corps was commanded by Gen. Lloyd Fredenhall[23] and later on by Gen. Omar Bradley.[24] The missions and practically the whole orientation of the XII Air Support Command were really to support the Army's II Corps. I think that accounts for the fact that we weren't going out hitting these airfields, and there was very little understanding of the importance of air superiority. If you will look at the people that were running the XII Air Support Command at the time, they actually had little experience in this sort of thing.

Ferguson: The Air Corps was an integral part of the Army at that time. The fledgling Air Corps was closely geared to ground action.

Momyer: There was very little perspective really of offensive air operations or fighter operations or this sort of thing. So I think the culmination was a kind of bubbling up, that something really had to be done if we were going to get control of the air. So, with the establishment of that Allied tactical air force [Northwest African Tactical Air Force], Air Vice Marshal Coningham came down to my airfield—at the time I was a colonel—and he said, "Colonel, the first thing we are going to do is get out and destroy the German air force. When we have destroyed the German Air Force in North Africa, we will do all the air support and anything else that the Army wants. But until we get those airfields and get those German airplanes off our back,

---

[22]The XII Air Support Command became part of the Twelfth Air Force in late 1943 as did the XII Fighter Command, the XII Troop Carrier Command, the 90th Photo Reonnaissance Wing, and training and service units. Led by Maj. Gen. James H. "Jimmy" Doolittle, the Twelfth Air Force had 1,244 aircraft assigned, compared with the RAF's 454 planes in North Africa. Even so, the American air forces were ineffective during the invasion of North Africa, a situation attributable to a lack of coordination between air and ground commanders. See Wesley F. Craven and James L. Cate, eds, *The Army Air Forces in World War II,* 7 vols (Chicago, 1948–58), Vol II: *Europe: Torch to Pointblank, August 1942 to December 1943,* 50–68.

[23]Lt. Gen. Lloyd R. Fredenhall (1883–1963). As a major general, he was selected by Lt. Gen. Dwight D. Eisenhower to direct the landing of U.S. forces at Oran, North Africa, during Operation Torch. The landing was successfully executed in November 1942, but Fredenhall drove his inexperienced forces eastward too rapidly and a diversionary offensive at Kasserine Pass led to an Allied disaster. Fredenhall was dismissed and replaced by Maj. Gen. George S. Patton, Jr.

[24]General of the Army Omar N. Bradley (1893–1981). After graduating from West Point in 1915, Bradley advanced through the ranks to major general in February 1942. When given the opportunity after the Kasserine Pass disaster, General Eisenhower selected Bradley as commander of the II Corps in late April 1943, succeeding General Patton who was picked to lead the invasion of Sicily. See Omar N. Bradley, *A Soldier's Story* (New York, 1951).

we are not going to do anything else." All this time a fight was going on between Patton and Coningham. Tedder was sent down because of the message that Patton sent with regards to the fact that he wasn't getting adequate air support. Eisenhower sent Tedder down to try to referee this, but it was all related to this fact that we didn't have control of the air.[25]

I think that kind of set the stage. General Quesada was up at the Coastal Air Force [Northwest African Coastal Air Force], and maybe he can give something from his perspective of what they were doing.

Quesada: You touched on a very interesting point which, I think, history has almost ignored. If there was a creator for the concept of tactical air operating in a manner that is removed somewhat from the Army, we have to say it was "Maori" Coningham. I will give you some of the history of that. Before we had landed in North Africa, the British had launched a great offensive, which was described as Alamein. Before that there was one hell of a fight between "Maori" Coningham and Montgomery.[26] Coningham was a very forceful fellow. He had a rather high squeaky voice; he was big of stature. His name was "Maori," and at times he had feminine gestures. But he was the most masculine man I think I have ever known. He was killed later. He was the only man in the RAF or anyplace that could stand up to Montgomery. When he stood up to Montgomery, as he did, in the most forceful manner, he won—as often happens (I hope all young officers

---

[25]An incident developed in early April 1943 in North Africa between General Patton, commander of the II Corps, U.S. Army, and RAF Air Vice Marshal Coningham, head of the Western Desert Air Force. In a situation report, Patton protested that a "total lack of air cover" had permitted the German air force to operate at will against his forces. His troops, he complained, had been "continuously bombed" all morning and every one of his command posts had been hit from the air. Coningham investigated and found that the air attacks had been exceptionally light, the number of casualties in Patton's army totaling six. That night Coningham sent a message to Patton, with information copies to Eisenhower and all higher headquarters, including London and Washington, accusing him of using the air forces "as an alibi for lack of success on the ground." Further, he asserted that his flyers in the future would not be put off by Patton's "false cry of wolf." Eisenhower, Allied commander in North Africa, was so disturbed at the bickering between his subordinates that he drafted a message to Army Chief of Staff Gen. George C. Marshall asking to be relieved of command. Fortunately Sir Arthur W. Tedder, RAF Air Chief Marshal and Coningham's superior, intervened and directed Coningham to apologize to Patton personally. He did, and the incident ended. See Lord Arthur Tedder, *With Prejudice: The War Memoirs of a Marshal of the Royal Air Force* (Boston, 1966), pp 410–14, and Stephen E. Ambrose, *The Supreme Commander: The War Years of Dwight David Eisenhower* (New York, 1970), pp 181–82.

[26]RAF Air Vice Marshal Sir Arthur Coningham was in 1942 the commander of the Western Desert Air Force. When Lt. Gen. Bernard L. Montgomery took command of the British Eighth Army in mid-August 1942, he moved quickly to consolidate army and air force headquarters. This move placed Coningham directly under Montgomery's control. The arguments that General Quesada refers to must have been brief, for by the time of the battle of El Alamein (October 24–November 5, 1942), Montgomery was fully committed to the air superiority doctrine. See Nigel Hamilton, *Monty: The Making of a General, 1887–1942* (New York, 1981), pp 638, 775–826.

remember this) if you stand up and pursue your convictions. It doesn't make any difference whom you are standing up to, you can win. You don't always win. But he stood up to Montgomery, and in the end Montgomery was Coningham's greatest admirer because he turned out to be right.

Alamein was the first time, if I recall correctly—I think you were there at Alamein, were you not?

Momyer: I was over on the other side. I remained in southern Tunisia at the time the breakthrough took place at El Alamein, and they started coming up....[27]

Quesada: I think Alamein took place before we went into Africa.

Momyer: October, I think, 1942.

Quesada: Okay. Nevertheless, "Maori" Coningham was the first senior air force guy who established tactical air doctrine as supportable doctrine which almost everybody accepted.[28] The doctrine that Spike has referred to: Coningham is the architect of it. He made everybody accept it, and almost everybody thereafter was forced to adopt it, and I think it should be recorded that he established it over tremendous opposition. He overcame the concept of using the air force as artillery, and he established the doctrine that if an airman is left to use his own weapon and use his experience he would further the cause of the army or the ground battle.

Ferguson: It is worth noting again that the RAF was a separate service at this point. On our side U.S. air was a corps of the Army and considered an extension of the field artillery. The lesson was absorbed by air leaders on the scene, and we were permitted to take the "half step" of forming tactical

---

[27]The battle of El Alamein, Egypt, lasted from October 24 to November 5, 1942. It engaged the British with 195,000 troops and 1,000 tanks against the Germans with 104,000 men and 500 tanks. Lt. Gen. Bernard L. Montgomery led the British to victory by shifting his attacking forces quickly and decisively at key moments in the battle to exploit weaknesses in Gen. Erwin Rommel's German lines. [Peter Calvocoressi and Guy Wint, *Total War: Causes and Courses of the Second World War* (London, 1972), pp 362–65; Charles K. Webster and Noble Frankland, *The Strategic Air Offensive Against Germany, 1939–1945*, 4 vols (London, 1961), I, 140–41, 201–9.]

[28]Immediately after the war the British United Services Institute, later known as the Royal United Services Institute, scheduled a monthly lecture on various aspects of the war. Air Marshal Sir Arthur Coningham's lecture, presented in February 1946, explained his concepts of air superiority, close air support, and interdiction. [Arthur Coningham, "The Development of Tactical Air Forces," *Journal of the United Services Institute* IX (1946), 211–27].

air forces geared to the actions of each field army. This was about the time you were in North Africa, Spike. It was many years after World War II, November 1947, that Congress authorized the establishment of the U.S. Air Force as a separate but equal military entity.

Lee: One interjection since we are talking about "Maori" Coningham. You brought to my mind that in the preparation of this first manual by Ralph Stearley and at General Arnold's direction, Stearley based this philosophy of control of the air, first as a prerequisite to proper air and ground operations, on...Coningham's philosophy, as I recall. It may not be in the notes where that manual is written, but I was there, and Stearley kept quoting Coningham all the time as he was writing this manual on control of the air. He used the word "control" because he thought air superiority was not exactly the right term but you need control of the air.*

Quesada: And control of the air in his mind—and it turned out to be right—included attacking the opponent's air power at its source.

Momyer: Where that was really put together, in the real formal document, was with the wind down of the Tunisian campaign and the two Allied forces joining together. Montgomery held this conference at Tripoli. The purpose of that conference in early 1943, if I recall correctly, was to review with his commanders the lessons of the Western Desert. That's when he gave his famous oration on the coequality of air: the airman commands forces that fly, the soldier commands forces on the ground, and the sailor commands forces that operate on the sea. It really became the whole basis later on of our doctrine. People kept saying what a wonderful thing that a soldier came out and made this statement. I have said this before. I was doing some research, and I went back through Air [Chief] Marshal Tedder's memoirs. Buried deep in his memoirs was the fact: no wonder Montgomery had given such an eloquent dissertation on air—Coningham had written it for him. The point was, it didn't make any difference who had written it; out of that came the basis, I think, of our first formalized doctrine.

---

*For FM 100–20, Command and Employment of Air Power, see Appendix.

Kuter[29] was a part of that whole process. Kuter came back at the time from North Africa, as you will recall, and made that the basis of the writing of the [Field Manual] 100–20. The 100–20 was really the emancipation proclamation, I call it, of air power, at least of tactical air power. It was the first time it was really set down in unequivocal terms as to the priority of missions. The first priority was to gain and maintain air superiority. The second priority was to isolate the battlefield. The third priority was to support the ground forces. That, I think then, you can say kind of summed up what came out of the North African campaign. Those three elements. For the first time, I think we had a doctrine that you could talk about in formalized terms and people could now see that this was the way it was going to be employed. That kind of set the stage for the invasion.

Ferguson: That was organization for the Normandy invasion—field army/tactical air command air-ground teams under Army group/Army Air Forces direction. The record shows how well this worked in Europe. In the Pacific the organizational relationship between air and ground was not so clear because of geographical considerations as well as personalities. Immediately after World War II, a joint Army-Navy board was convened in Washington to record lessons of air and ground coordination and to draft joint doctrine. I was a member of this board chosen, perhaps, because I spent the last few months of the war in the Pacific trying to explain and to help organize the air and ground coordination procedures as we conducted them in Europe. During the heat of battle, we improvised and made things work, but when the fighting was over, service prerogatives quickly came to the surface, and we made little progress in coming to any agreement. I don't think that draft report was ever finalized.

Momyer: And I think that will go on indefinitely. My theory is that air power is so flexible that everybody wants a part of it.

Kohn: Are you saying, in effect, that despite all the arguments and all the thinking of the twenty years between the wars, what really decided these

---

[29]Gen. Laurence S. Kuter (1905–79). A graduate of West Point in 1927, Kuter served during World War II as a planner in the Air War Plans Division, a bomber pilot, commander of the 1st Bombardment Wing, Eighth Air Force, and Assistant Chief of Air Staff, Plans, Army Air Forces. For an review of Kuter's career, see interview (K239.0512–810), Thomas A. Sturm, Office of Air Force History, and Hugh N. Ahmann, Albert F. Simpson Historical Research Center, with Gen. Laurence S. Kuter, USAF, Retired, Naples, Florida, October 7–10, 1974.

issues and drew them out was the joining of forces and the reality of combat—that on the one hand, and on the other the strength and vision of the airman (you mentioned Air Marshal Coningham) seeing combat and imposing solutions in the situation?

Momyer: Perseverance and the hard lessons of what was seen, what was happening, the fact that your force was being attrited. You saw that you weren't accomplishing what you set out to do. The strength of the personalities involved and the fact that some people had the foresight to put this down, to start synthesizing it, were all factors. And I think, furthermore, the same thing was translated for the commanders who were on the verge of the invasion. They had a pretty good idea, and I think they took it up from there and put it into the planning that went into the air operations for the invasion.

Quesada: Another way you can express what he is saying and you are saying is that in the second World War necessity and experience resulted in an evolution. Our doctrine evolved. The doctrine that evolved was the doctrine that Spike and all of us are referring to.

Ferguson: The Eagle squadrons of the RAF included many young American pilots. Some returned to the United States early and visited our training centers to pass on their experiences. Spike, I don't think you were in that group, but you were part of the U.S. effort to learn from RAF experience. I had a fighter training wing in Florida producing pilots for duty in North Africa and the South Pacific. The early combat experiences of the Eagle squadron pilots were invaluable in modifying our training programs to the realities of current combat scenarios.[30] Another small step in our transition from World War I to World War II.

Momyer: I think there is a lesson there that stands out. Obviously there is no substitute for combat. That's where you develop your leaders; you develop the understanding. In between wars, it seems to me, wherever anybody else has got a war, we certainly ought to have the best people we

---

[30]During World War II, the Royal Air Force had three squadrons manned exclusively with American pilots. Some 240 American pilots joined the squadrons in 1940 and 1941 and participated in the Battle of Britain and other air engagements. In September 1942 the squadrons, with all of their personnel, transferred to the U.S. Army Air Forces. See Vern Haugland, *The Eagle Squadrons: Yanks in the RAF, 1940–1942* (New York, 1979).

The three-place 0-47 observation aircraft, which General Lee believes could not survive in the air against contemporary fighters.

have in the business there watching and analyzing and digesting what's going on, trying to translate that experience into the current way that we do things. I think that process was probably one of our biggest failures between the world wars, because there were a number of lesser wars going on in the 1930s—for example, the Ethiopian war.[31] Almost anywhere that you could turn, there were wars going on sometime. There were bits and pieces, it would seem to me, that were coming out of these things, but there was no one synthesizing and saying, "Well, what are the meanings of all these little pieces coming together?" That is probably a lesson that we could well digest. This is different than having the intelligence people do it. I am not talking about the formalized intelligence observation. I am talking about the people who are going to be responsible for the operations and the training and the planning. Those kinds of things.

---

[31]Benito Mussolini, Fascist leader of Italy, sent Italian army and air forces into Ethiopia in October 1935. This Italian invasion was a war of conquest in which Ethiopia was defeated quickly and then incorporated into an Italian empire. From 1935 to 1941 Ethiopia was a colony of Italy. When World War II began in Europe, former Ethiopian Emperor Haile Selassie organized nationalist forces and drove the Italians out of the country. With British support, he achieved victory in May 1941. [Richard Greenfield, *Ethiopia: A New Political History* (New York, 1965), pp 199–223, 251–265; Denis M. Smith, *Mussolini's Roman Empire* (New York, 1977).]

Lee: One more little item that is not thought of much in pre-World War II is observation and recce type of operations. About 1940 I happened to take an observation squadron, [12th Observation Squadron] which was equipped with O–43s and later O–47s, and organized it from cadres. It became the 10th Recce Wing [10th Reconnaissance Group], which you finally got down in 19th Tac [XIX Tactical Air Command]. As I say, the development of an observation airplane gave no consideration whatsoever to enemy air, air superiority, or control of the air. Those planes had a tail gun which probably wasn't worth anything, but they considered them-selves able to go around almost unhindered and take pictures and make observations and spot artillery and so forth. During the time that I had my squadron, we got O–47s, a three-place airplane with a pilot, a gunner, and a fellow who could sit up on top or lay down in the belly and take pictures or look. It was obvious to me that thing would never survive. Having had pursuit experience, I felt we needed an airplane which could survive in the air. Therefore, on my own, I went up to Wright Field [Ohio] looking for some type of fighter airplane. I was at Godman Field, Fort Knox, Ken-tucky, at the time, and Dayton [Ohio] was pretty handy. I was sent around to the project officers for various fighter airplanes. The P–38 [Lightning] was already tied up in both fighter and some recce type activities. The P–47 project officer was all tied up in his airplane, and they weren't interested in trying to make a recce airplane out of it. I finally went to the P–51 [Mustang] fellow. There was a little second lieutenant there who told me that there were some Mustangs with low-altitude engines that the British had ordered which they didn't want, and he thought maybe we could get them. I was thinking about putting packages of some sort on the things. So I went back and made this report and said we would like to try them out. Son of a gun, if we didn't get eighteen of these aircraft for a squadron. By this time, I had taken some time getting additional Lightnings for this group, and we got a full squadron of these Lightnings and put some packages on the airplanes in the place of the wing tanks. I had one squadron equipped with those down in Louisiana. They were low altitude, which fitted our purpose quite well. It was merely a trial down at Esler Field [Louisiana], I think it was, where we had these Mustangs. Everybody reported favorably, and out of that developed the F–6, which was a P–51 with dicing cameras and wing camera packages. That also shows the requirement, as it de-veloped then, for some recce airplane which could, instead of flying around in peacetime taking pictures, survive in the air. In fact they had guns on them, and you people down at 19th Tac had to order them to quit shooting German airplanes.[32]

Kohn: Prior to the war, were design and performance standards for our air superiority aircraft—indeed any kind of aircraft—being primarily determined by pilots' desires or by designers? Was there so much of a separation that when the doctrine evolved, as you have described it, you were left with aircraft that had to be constantly modified for any mission?

Momyer: Maybe we have done a little bit of an injustice, but you really had three phases of aviation at the time prior to World War II. You had the pursuit. As we have discussed, pursuit was primarily oriented for air defense and so-called bomber escort, not really for offensive employment for what we would call today going out and engaging and destroying the air force. Pursuit as such was designed with no capabilities to attack ground targets. So I think that is the first point.

Secondly, you had bombardment, and bombardment was primarily tailored, as we have mentioned, for strategic operations.

Third, you had attack aviation, which we haven't even talked about. Attack aviation was primarily the force that was going to go down and do the support of the ground forces and do this other type of mission.

Finally, you had the observation, and the observation was primarily tailored to the ground forces.

Lee: The airplane was built more or less to specification for the mission—the mission oriented for taking pictures for the ground forces and spotting artillery.

Momyer: I think then on the edge of World War II, we were really specialized to those functions.

Kohn: Not multipurpose aircraft?

Momyer: I think that's what we are going to see as we get into North Africa. One of the things that came out of the North African campaign, for example, from my own experience, was that a P–40 was designed within

---

[32]The Ninth and Twelfth Air Forces furnished tactical air support for Lt. Gen. Omar N. Bradley's 12th Army Group in its movement across France, Belgium, and Germany.

the concept that I have just said. But it wasn't very long till we were hanging bombs on P–40s, and it wasn't very long, for example, till the Hurricane, which was designed for the air defense of Great Britain, had bombs hanging on it. They were out doing attack of airfields and the same thing. So really out of the North African campaign, not only was the doctrine switching, but the concept of fighter aviation was switching. We were getting off of pursuit as being a relatively limited aircraft only for air defense purposes and going to a flexible fighter that could be used for counterair operations, for the attack of airfields, for the attack of lines of communication, and for close air support of ground forces. I think that came out of the North African campaign, and we will see, as World War II started to unfold in Europe, the true versatility of the force that began to be employed to these functions.

Ferguson: I was going to make a point in response to one of your questions about the influence of engineers or pilots on the design of airplanes. The governing factor, I think, was more technology: what was possible to build in those days in terms of powerplants and what we knew about aerodynamics and structures. That was the transition, if you look at the performance of airplanes from the end of World War I down to the end of World War II. We had the P–1, P–6, P–16, P–12, later the P–26, and then the P–36. But they were really just projections of technology, more so than aircraft oriented to any specific mission. When World War II descended on us, we had some adaptations to make. The P–40 was supposed to be an air-to-air fighter, and I had one of the first squadrons of P–40Fs. One day we decided we ought to try some ground attack with it, and all hell descended on us from Washington. That was an air-to-air fighter as it was bought.

Kohn: Can we now switch from North Africa to Europe? Let me pose a paradox to you. You have described the North African campaign: air superiority won by air-to-air combat, attacks against airfields, AAA, and the lines of communication. The history books tell us that the way we gained air superiority over France and Germany was to attack the German homeland, attack the aircraft industry, and then draw up the German air force and shoot the aircraft out of the sky. Was there a different lesson to be learned in air superiority fighting the Germans over France and over Germany, or was there a natural evolution from the North African campaign? Were these two campaigns so different that we are dealing with a different question here, a different facet of air superiority?

Towards multipurpose aircraft: Pre-World War II aircraft were designed for specific purposes. The Keystone B-6s (above) were built to drop bombs on ground targets. However, as a result of the North African campaign, P-40s (below) were often equipped with bombs and used in attacking airfields and for supporting ground forces, in addition to their traditional air-to-air fighter role. A bomb rack was installed on a P-6 (adjacent page) as well as on P-40s originally designed for air-to-air combat.

Quesada: Let me take a crack at that. My observations are borne of a little bit of experience as I was in England during the Battle of Britain and afterwards. This is the first time I have ever thought of it or thought it through like I am now going to try to think it through. The concept you referred to occurred during the Battle of Britain and after. What I think brought it about—I am being intuitive now—was that the British saw how the Germans failed. The Germans nearly won that war, and the British, I think, knew quite well that the Germans damn near won it. Had the Germans kept attacking targets in England that the British would have had to come up and defend, and had the Germans sent fighters over to bring the British into combat, then Germany would perhaps have had air superiority over England. So I intuitively think both England and ourselves (they confronted the problem, and we observed it) realized how important it was.

43

If you are going to attack an enemy, you have to make their air force come up and fight. You have to attack targets that will make them commit their air force to fight. So I am inclined to think in retrospect, either consciously or unconsciously, that the philosophy resulted from the Germans' failure to employ it. The Germans were so close to the target—it was much easier for them than us, operating out of England. If they had had sense enough, or the brilliance enough, to conduct their offensive, which was sort of half-assed as it now is revealed, against England to make them come up and fight to defend essential targets as occurred two years later over Germany, I think Germany might have won.

Momyer: I think there is really a very basic difference in views during the strategic air campaign prior to the time of the invasion, or prior to the buildup for the invasion. The strategic air campaign really viewed air superiority as being a byproduct of destroying German potential to wage war. If you will look at the priority list, the German Air Force per se was a relatively low priority.

Quesada: Almost not included, almost not included, initially.

Momyer: I think this was later modified. I really think the opposite view in essence says: In order to prosecute that kind of a campaign, you must destroy the air force; otherwise, the attrition is going to be so high, unless you are using different types of weapons than conventional weapons, that you simply can't sustain that type of an operation. There was a fundamental difference. With the coming of the invasion, there was a definite shift, as you well know, and you [General Quesada] did a lot of the planning. The planning was to destroy the German Air Force so that it couldn't actively challenge the invasion. You remember that Spaatz and Harris and the rest were hollering: "Don't take us off of the strategic campaign. Give us some more time. If you give us a little bit more time, we are going to be able to wind the war down." The other people—Eisenhower—had the commitment that the bombers would come under his command, and definitely for that three-month campaign, the German Air Force was the primary effort, except for interdiction.[33]

---

[33]Maj. Gen. Carl A. Spaatz, Eighth Air Force commander, and Air Chief Marshal Arthur T. Harris, commander of the RAF Bomber Command, led the Allied air forces that were committed to the Combined Bomber Offensive against Germany. During the intense planning and marshaling of forces

Quesada: In everybody's mind the German Air Force was the primary target. I don't know whether it was written down, and I am having a hard time trying to find out where it came from. I think one of the people that contributed to it in a mighty way was "Fred"Anderson.[34]

Momyer: Hansell.[35]

Quesada: And perhaps Hansell, too, "Possum" Hansell.

Momyer: Hansell was one of the basic theorists in this whole business, and he believes that today really. If you would talk to him today, I think you would get the same viewpoint.

Quesada: There was a definite surge of thought, often opposed, that established that the way to make the strategic force really effective was to defeat the enemy air force first. It was not universally accepted.

---

for the invasion of Normandy, Spaatz and Harris objected strenuously to the diversion of strategic bombers and skilled aircrews from the long-range strategic bombing missions over Germany to interdiction missions over western France. The controversy flared into intense debate in Allied circles in February–March 1944. At one point or another, discussions involved the top leadership of both the British and American forces, including Prime Minister Winston Churchill. Finally, General Eisenhower decided to divert the bombers for a three-month campaign against railheads and communications centers in France. See Wesley F. Craven and James L. Cate, eds, *The Army Air Forces in World War II*, 7 vols (Chicago, 1948–58), Vol III: *Europe: Argument to V–E Day, January 1944 to May 1945*, 72–79; Haywood S. Hansell, Jr., *The Air Plan That Defeated Hitler* (Atlanta, Ga., 1972), pp 186–192; W. W. Rostow, *Pre-Invasion Bombing Strategy: General Eisenhower's Decision of 25 March 1944* (Austin, Tex., 1981).

[34]Maj. Gen. Frederick L. Anderson, Jr. (1905–69). Anderson worked closely with Maj. Gen. Ira C. Eaker, commander of the Eighth Air Force, and RAF Air Chief Marshal Sir Charles Portal in mid–1943 in devising the strategic bombing plan against Germany. This plan became the operational guide for the Combined Bomber Offensive launched in June 1943. Anderson worked directly with Brig. Gen. Haywood S. Hansell, Jr., director of the AAF planning team. See Haywood S. Hansell, Jr., *The Air Plan That Defeated Hitler* (Atlanta, Ga., 1972), p 152.

[35]Maj. Gen. Haywood S. Hansell, Jr. (1903–) entered the Air Corps in 1928 as a flying cadet. After training and flying with Capt. Claire L. Chennault, an innovator in developing pursuit tactics, Hansell taught tactics at the Air Corps Tactical School. There he developed a strong interest in strategic bombing concepts and early in World War II was chief of the European Branch of the Air War Plans Division, Army Air Forces. Moving to the European theater in late 1942, Hansell commanded the 1st and 3d Bombardment Wings, Eighth Air Force. In mid–1943 Hansell became the deputy to RAF Air Chief Marshal Sir Trafford Leigh-Mallory, commander in chief of the Allied Expeditionary Air Force. There he was intimately involved in the planning session for the Combined Bomber Offensive against Germany. In 1944 Hansell became Chief of Staff, Twentieth Air Force, and then went to the Pacific and took command of the XXI Bomber Command, equipped with B–29s. In January 1945 Gen. Henry H. Arnold replaced him with Maj. Gen. Curtis E. LeMay. In 1946 Hansell retired from the Army Air Forces for physical disability. He returned to active duty during the Korean War. For a statement of Hansell's strategic view, see Haywood S. Hansell, Jr., *The Air Plan That Defeated Hitler* (Atlanta, Ga., 1972).

Momyer: LeMay's expression was, "A determined bomber offensive was never turned back."[36] I think that's an oversimplification, but it's an expression of the concept that you could drive bombers through, and you really didn't have to beat down the enemy air force in order to get in there. You will do that by destroying things—his fuel and everything else needed to put his air force up and sustain it.

Lee: The pure strategic philosophy was to go after the basic industry and things like that, which, as Spike has said, would draw up the air force, you might say, as a by product. You would certainly have some air-to-air, but the bombers didn't have escort initially. They would go in and use their own guns for defense but I don't think primarily to defeat the air force. As Pete says, the airfields were not initially on the target list as far as I can tell.

Quesada: Absolutely.

Kohn: Let me ask you, General Quesada, the lesson learned, as you have thought it through now, that comes from the Battle of Britain and Germany's failure in the Battle of Britain. In 1942 and 1943, if I remember correctly, we were still thinking we would fight our way through, almost in a bubble of air superiority, into the targets and then back. Perhaps operations—am I right or wrong here—had not yet caught up, in 1942 and 1943, to the lesson learned in 1940–41.

Quesada: You have it exactly right. Let me digress and speculate: If Germany had equipped itself to implement the concept of air superiority over the target in 1940 and 1941 as we evolved it in 1942 and 1943, I think they would have brought England to its knees.

Momyer: I think the German concept was proper; it just wasn't pursued.

Quesada: Wasn't pursued, and they didn't quite have that....

---

[36]Gen. Curtis E. LeMay (1906–). In the 1950s LeMay built the Strategic Air Command into the dominant, long-range, strategic air arm. During World War II, he led a series of bomber units in Europe for the Eighth Air Force before becoming commander of the XX Bomber Command at Kharagpur, India, and later of the XXI Bomber Command at Harmon Field, Guam. As XXI commander he developed the tactics and plans for B–29 missions which firebombed Tokyo. When World War II ended, LeMay returned to the United States as Deputy Chief/Air Staff, Research and Development, AAF. In October 1948 he became commander in chief of Strategic Air Command. For a discussion of LeMay's concept of strategic bombing, see Curtis E. LeMay and MacKinlay Kantor, *Mission with LeMay: My Story* (New York, 1965).

Momyer: They had the concept, but they really hadn't thought it through to its logical conclusions, and they didn't have the courage of their convictions to pursue it. Actually they started out with bringing the RAF fighter command up to engage and suffer attrition; they also went at the airfields, at the radars and command and control. Their whole concept was that they could gain air superiority in a relatively short period of time. Adolf Hitler wasn't willing really to pursue that, and he shifted the target system. When he shifted to the ports, he shifted to targets that initially had to be neutralized before invading. That premature shift, I think, is the thing really. If the German air force had pursued the same sort of doctrine as in Poland, the same sort of doctrine that had been pursued in France, which was to gain air superiority over the battlefield—and the same thing that had been pursued in the first campaigns against the Soviet Union—the outcome in the Battle of Britain might have been different.

Lee: Does anybody have anything to say about what certain historians have said: that Hitler had a certain spot in his heart for England and suddenly just called off the bombing when he did it?

Quesada: I think he called it off because he was licked.

Lee: You think he did it, or did his military people? He sort of ran things, you know.

Momyer: If you go back—at least I haven't been able to find anything like a detailed air plan for the invasion of England. At best it appears as an ad hoc operation. As systematic as they had been about planning for the ground operations, their air planning was really atrocious. It's really remarkable, and I think for this very short period of time, the attrition rates went up, went up very high. As a consequence, they backed off, and then they started to go at the ports and thought the British would collapse because of that. But they didn't. As a consequence, the Germans were into an attrition campaign, and they didn't feel they could sustain it.

Quesada: Let me recite a little piece of trivia, and forgive me if a slight personal note is injected in it. When the buildup of our Air Force in England was under way and before the actual invasion and the strategic envelopment was building up and becoming gargantuan, P–47s, P–38s, and P–51s were arriving in England. The tactical air forces, the tactical air commands, were mine at the time—that's the personal note that I have to use. I don't like to use the personal pronoun; nevertheless, all the P–51s were assigned to us. Maybe you all don't know that—everyone of them, every P–51 group. Now we had about four months to go before landing in Normandy. To have those people standing by and doing nothing, waiting for the landing, would have been just ridiculous. So everybody, including me, was more than glad to have those planes support the Eighth Air Force. The first deep penetrations that occurred into Germany by massive B–17 formations were to Kiel. The P–51s and others flew across the channel and escorted the bombers to Kiel. There was a battle over Kiel every day for about four or five days. The P–51 won every battle. The P–51 turned out to be able to slaughter the German fighters. The odds were great. One guy shot down five in one day. What was that guy's name?

Ferguson: Howard.[37]

Quesada: Yes, Howard in the 356th [Fighter] Squadron.

Ferguson: His group was the 354th.

Quesada: The 354th [Fighter] Group, right....Howard was the group commander. Anyway that's beside the point. It was then, and not until then, that it was totally realized and proven that the P–51 could go farther and fight better. Now something occurred. People said: "Look, maybe it's a bad assignment to have the P–51s assigned to the tactical air forces when they were so superior in the role of defending the strategic air forces and making the Germans fight. "That was so evident to me that I didn't resist a goddamn bit. Everybody thought I was going to resist like hell. I don't know whether you know that or not, but a lot of the aircraft (the groups remained), the P–51s, were assigned to the Eighth Air Force's newly arriving groups and more P–47s to us. It was just so obvious, so apparent to

---

[37]Brig. Gen. James H. Howard (1913–). A Medal of Honor winner, Howard joined the American Volunteer Group of the Chinese air force in August 1941. Led by Claire L. Chennault, the American Flying Tigers flew intercept missions against the Japanese air force. Howard shot down six enemy fighters and a bomber in the eleven months that he served with Chennault and the Flying Tigers. Transferring to the European theater in 1943, he commanded the 356th Fighter Squadron, Ninth Air Force. He led his P–51 squadron on long-range missions, accompanying B–17 and B–24 bombers across the North Sea to Germany. Many of these raids were to Kiel, Germany, a naval dockyard for submarines and a naval production center for the manufacture of torpedoes. During the Combined Bomber Offensive, British and American bombers attacked Kiel using radar-bombing techniques. [Wesley F. Craven and James L. Cate, eds, *The Army Air Forces in World War II,* 7 vols (Chicago, 1948–58), Vol III: *Europe: Argument to V–E Day, January 1944 to May 1945,* 19–21.]

Maj. Gen. Elwood R. Quesada (right) in the cockpit of a P-38, England, 1944. Mustang fighters (below) proved to be supreme in escorting bombers to targets deep in German territory.

anybody with any objectivity at all—and don't think I didn't hate to lose them. I hated to lose them. But I didn't raise my finger. Do you remember that, Bob?

Lee: You kept two groups, though. The 354th and one other.

Quesada: Because we had to do some fighting. Well, I am not that objective. Those battles over Kiel contributed to the accepted philosophy that we will fight them in the air and wear them down because success was evident. The P–51 made people think we could go in farther and farther and win and win.

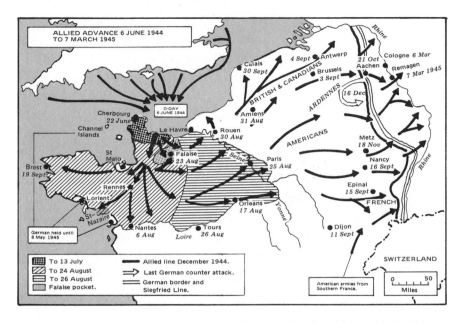

Victory in Europe depended on the success of the Normandy invasion, which was launched with the assault landing on 6 June 1944. The English Channel presented the most difficult barrier to the invasion because of navigational hazards and extreme tidal variations along the French coast. This placed a severe burden on control of air power. Once firmly ashore, however, there would be ample opportunity and freedom of maneuver for ground forces driving to the German heartland.

Ferguson: I would like to add just a little bit to that. I took a P–47 group to England several months before the Normandy invasion. As D–Day approached, some of us were ordered to the RAF 11th Group—the center which would control all the air forces, United States and United Kingdom—during the invasion. Until then we prepared the field orders for U.S. bomber and fighter groups in coordination with RAF operations. When deep penetrations were made by the bombers, as in the case of Berlin which was six hundred miles, fighter groups were assigned segments of the route in and out to cover the bombers. To do this fighters had to use external fuel tanks which were dropped in the event of air engagement—full or empty. This carefully planned operation could have easily been upset had the Germans intercepted the bomber stream early in the penetration of the Continent. Fighters would have had to drop their tanks to engage, thus shortening their endurance and forcing an early return which could leave the bombers without cover on a portion of their route—highly vulnerable to enemy fighters. It could have been very serious; fortunately the Luftwaffe staff didn't see this opportunity.

Looking back over these operations, we see what might be called an inversion in the use of fighters and bombers—further testimony to the flexibility of airpower. In Europe we considered a target out to six hundred miles as strategic; fighters seldom ranged beyond three hundred for ground attack. Yet, when we looked at Spike's more recent experience in Vietnam, we saw B–52s hitting close-in targets and fighters doing the deep penetrations.

Momyer: I would like to ask General Quesada a $64 question. When Eisenhower had made his decision some months prior to the invasion, what kind of assessment was made that you could tell him, "We will have control of the air, and there is no question about our ability to control the air so that your invasion can take place"? These kinds of gut issues keep coming up. People keep asking me—and I didn't want to get into Vietnam—but they keep asking me these kinds of questions as if there is a scientific answer. There is no scientific answer to this. It's a combination of a lot of things. I am sure you will bring it out, too, but it's a combination of your experience and everything else.

Quesada: That was an issue, and that answer was given to Eisenhower. My memory tells me it was given to him because of experience. We were confident that we could knock the hell out of the German Air Force wherever it was. We were confident that the interdiction program would succeed and that the German Air Force, in terms of Normandy, couldn't be very close to it because if they did deploy close to Normandy—which they didn't, which all of us now know—we could knock the hell out of them. We were confident that our effort against the German Air Force, over Berlin or wherever it was, would succeed. Every commander who was involved in the damn thing was totally confident.

Momyer: It was a collective judgment?

Quesada: Well, I don't know about that. I think there might have been some doubters.

Ferguson: I will tell you, the only German airplanes that were seen on D–Day were by the RP–51s that went way in as far as they could go.

Momyer: Yes, I know. The Germans flew only 750 sorties as the total amount of effort, but they had a significant amount of air force still left. The question really comes up: How were we so confident? What was the basis of this judgment? What made you think they really weren't going to be able to mount a last-ditch effort? After all, this was the invasion of their homeland, and if they didn't stop it, the war was over.

Kohn: Was it your numbers of aircraft, General Quesada, or your quality of your aircraft, or both?

Quesada: Both. There is another point. The quality of the German Air Force was visibly diminishing, and we were having such success—the Eighth Air Force fighters and the Ninth Air Force fighters that were contributing. Anytime they would meet the German Air Force, they would do it with success. It was quite obvious. As time went on, the opposition was getting less and less. I will tell you a little anecdote which goes back to Spike's question. His question really was, how was Eisenhower convinced that this could succeed? He had to be confident months ahead of the incident that I will relate.

About four days before D–Day, there was a briefing with the prime minister.[38] Each of the commanders who were going to participate in it was there. So I was tagging along. Being somewhat brash and also somewhat young (which made me brash), there came up in the course of my presentation (and I can't remember whether it was an Englishman or an American who asked—I have the recollection that it was an American, either Gerow[39] or "Joe" Collins,[40] both corps commanders), I was asked, "How are you going to keep the German Air Force from preventing our landing?" I said, "General, there is not going to be any German Air Force there."

"Ahhh," the prime minister spoke up. I think he said something to the effect, "Young man, how can you be so sure?" I said, "Mr. Prime Minister, experience tells us that wherever we have met the German Air Force over the last six months, we have defeated them. The German Air

---

[38]Prime Minister Winston Churchill.

[39]Gen. Leonard T. Gerow (1888–1972). As a major general (later a lieutenant general), Gerow commanded V Corps, First Army, which landed on Omaha Beach, Normandy on June 6, 1944. Subsequently, Gerow's corps fought for the liberation of Paris, France, and then through northern France, Belgium, and into Germany.

[40]Gen. J. Lawton Collins (1896–). As a major general (later a lieutenant general), Collins led the VII Corps, First Army, which went ashore on June 6, 1944, at Utah Beach, Normandy, France. The VII Corps led the Allied armies en masse in Normandy out of the beachhead area in the critical breakout battle of Saint-Lo in July 1944. Subsequently, this Army corps fought across France, Belgium, and Germany, stopping at the Elbe River in Germany in April 1945.

Lt. Gen. Carl A. Spaatz, in the planning for the invasion of Normandy, is surrounded by: (l. to r.) Maj. Gen. Ralph C. Royce, Maj. Gen. Hoyt S. Vandenberg, and Maj. Gen. Hugh J. Knerr.

Force today, Mr. Prime Minister, is impotent, and there will be no German Air Force over the Normandy invasion area." I never will forget it. The static in the room was knocking the ceiling off.

Momyer: You didn't have any of the kinds of problems with "tools" that they use today: that X percentage of the airfields had to be knocked out and X number of sorties had to be reduced before you had control of the air. [Laughter.]

Quesada: I might say, and this is only an anecdote: After the war when Eisenhower was president, the prime minister came over and was staying at the White House. I was a special assistant to Eisenhower at the time, and there was a dinner. After the dinner everybody was sitting around, and the prime minister was sitting there, and I was sitting beside him just chatting.

He said, "Young man, I remember you. You are the young man that told me there would be no German Air Force over Normandy." He remembered it, because it was brash; it was of youth and ego, I guess.

Ferguson: There is one other little anecdote that could be inserted here. General Quesada was the air advisor to General Eisenhower and the commander of all the tactical air forces for the invasion, which was set for—what was it? The fifth of June?

Quesada: The fifth that's right.

Ferguson: All the troops had been put into vessels, and they were all ready to go from Saint Catherine's Point on the south of England across to the Normandy beachhead. The weather people had great difficulty with their forecasts. The night before the invasion, the decision was made to postpone twenty-four hours. I must say the distinguished gentleman to my left was not quite so brash that night. He was really on pins and needles about what was going to happen. Because if you delayed more than twenty-four hours, what was it going to be? Another year's delay perhaps?

Quesada: Another moon.

Ferguson: It was a very tricky operation. Of course, we went across the next morning and with marginal weather.

Momyer: Who did the planning as far as the air planning?

Ferguson: The 11th Group, RAF, but it was a joint U.S./RAF group that wrote the daily operations orders.

Quesada: I think it is better to say you did the execution. The planning was done—what was the name of that place, Bob?

Lee: It was up at High Wycombe. [England]

Quesada: No. All the planning, American and British, was done in one place, and I can't remember the name of the place. I have to say in retrospect that the planning was incredibly intelligent. It really was. That headquarters was in existence a year before we started assembling in England.

54

Lee: I think it was Stanmore [England] because the British would say, "I have got to send a signal to Stanmore."

Quesada: All the planning of the basic invasion, where we would go, was all done in one place.

Lee: Allied Expeditionary Air Force was the name of the ———

Momyer: Did Leigh-Mallory's[41] headquarters do all the planning as far as the air planning?

Quesada: No.

Momyer: Well, that's what I am really trying to get. What was the role of the———

Quesada: I think you have to draw a distinction between the planning and the execution.

Momyer: I am talking about execution.

Quesada: You are talking about execution?

Lee: That was Leigh-Mallory.

Quesada: Because at that time he commanded all of the tactical air forces, both British and American, and he was trying to get the strategic air forces. With Leigh-Mallory, that's where the planning was done.

---

[41]In the preparations for the Normandy invasion, an important distinction had been drawn between planning and executing the operation. RAF Air Chief Marshal Sir Trafford Leigh-Mallory had been selected as commander in chief of the Allied Expeditionary Air Force. Leigh-Mallory and his joint British-American staff planned the air campaign, known as the "Transportation Plan," for the Normandy invasion. This planning group was headquartered at Stanmore, England, near London. In contrast, General Eisenhower's operational staff was located at Bushy Park, London, several miles distant from Stanmore. Eisenhower's deputy for air operations was RAF Air Chief Marshal Sir Arthur W. Tedder. [Wesley F. Craven and James L. Cate, eds, *The Army Air Forces in World War II*, 7 vols (Chicago, 1948–58), Vol III: *Europe: Argument to V–E Day, January 1944 to May 1945*, 67–69; Maurice Matloff and Edwin M. Snell, *Strategic Planning for Coalition Warfare, 1941–1942* [U.S. Army in World War II: The War Department], (Washington, 1953), pp 404–8.]

Momyer: That's why Tedder nominally exercised operational control of the strategic forces for the invasion, in which he was Eisenhower's deputy, because they didn't want to put the strategic air forces under the control of Leigh-Mallory.

Quesada: That's correct.

On that briefing that I referred to when the prime minister was there—that may have been a Thursday or a Wednesday; nevertheless, on the weekend following it, the prime minister invited about a dozen of the guys that would be involved in the actual landing in Normandy down to Chequers, which is the country home of the prime minister. I was tagging along, and the form was: you left London at about 4:30 and got there about 5:30; then you had tea; then you would go upstairs and take a shower and perhaps a little nap; then you would come down to a man's dinner. There is nothing more delightful than an Englishman's dinner. A man's dinner English-style is very formal The table was an oak table like that. There were no more than twelve there, and I was trying to get another LST [landing ship, tank] from the admiral on my right, and the general on my left was trying to get some more air support for his division. The conversation was very low key. You talked only on the right and only on the left.

At the opposite end of the table was the prime minister's son-in-law . . . that very few people know about.[42] In this subdued conversation and toward the end of dinner, the son-in-law called up the table and said, "Pops." Christ, to have the prime minister referred to as "Pops" is going to attract your attention, because the military people adored the prime minister. He was marvelous. The prime minister said, "Yes, my son?" The son-in-law said, "Would you give us a hand at this end of the table?" "I will try." "We are trying to decide who is the greatest living statesman of our time." Now we all got eloquent. Without a moment of hesitation, the prime minister roared, "Mussolini." "Well, why do you say that, Pops?" "The only statesman of our time with sufficient courage to murder his own son-in-law." I will never forget that as long as I live. I just couldn't believe it.

Kohn: Let me ask just one last question about World War II. To what degree did the achievement of air superiority depend on Ultra, breaking of

[42]Duncan Edwin Sandys married Diana Churchill in 1935. He served as finance member of the Army Council for much of World War II.

the German codes and the reading of their signal messages throughout the European theater?[43]

Quesada: I don't know of anybody here other than myself that had Ultra available. Did you have Ultra available?

Lee: Yes.

Ferguson: We had Y–service.[44]

Quesada: I would say that Ultra had a profound effect on air superiority in a rather oblique way. I think the real effect of Ultra was to instill in the very highest command—I don't mean myself but Eisenhower, the prime minister, the president, to a lesser extent Bradley—to have confidence in what they were doing. If the Germans meant what they were saying through Ultra, I think the attitude was, "We must be doing something right." I assure you that Ultra didn't permit us to do something tomorrow. You were not allowed to respond to Ultra tomorrow. If you did you would get your ass kicked out of the theater so fast it would make your head swim. I would say the real effect of Ultra was to instill confidence and provide guidance to the conduct of the war, if I may put it in those terms, rather than the tactics of the war.

Momyer: Do you really think it had a significant effect, though, on the disposition of your forces and the actual employment of your forces? The

---

[43]During World War II the Germans used an encryption machine called Enigma. The British, assisted by the Polish and French, broke the code for Enigma and extracted the intelligence data which they labeled Top Secret Ultra. This Ultra intelligence data went to a few political leaders and military commanders. For the greater part of the war, German Enigma messages were systematically, regularly, and extensively deciphered. See Peter Calvocoressi, *Top Secret Ultra* (New York, 1981); Ronald Lewin, *Ultra Goes to War* (New York, 1978); and the official British history by Francis H. Hinsley, *et al, British Intelligence in the Second World War: Its Influence on Strategy and Operations,* 2 vols (London, 1979–81). For a survey of the literature on Ultra and its impact on the study of World War II, see David Syrett, "The Secret War and the Historians," *Armed Forces and Society,* 9, (1983), 293–328.

[44]Throughout World War II the British operated a "Y–service," consisting of men and women from the army, navy, and air force. Essentially the people assigned to the Y–service operated intercept stations where they recorded German voice (radio) and signal (wireless) traffic. Initiated in England in the midst of the Battle of Britain, the Y–service expanded considerably during the war, finally encompassing much of western Europe, North Africa, Middle East, and the Atlantic Ocean area. The Germans also operated a top secret Y–service. [Calvocoressi, *Top Secret Ultra,* pp 41–44; Anthony Cave Brown, *Bodyguard of Lies* (New York, 1975), pp 35–36, 40–41, 495–99, 520–21, 549–550; Hinsley, *et al, British Intelligence in the Second World War: Its Influence on Strategy and Operations,* 2 vols (London, 1979–81), I, 327–28, 559–561.]

The Allies' "Ultra Secret": As early as 1939, the British had acquired a copy of the German encryption device known as Enigma (above). With help from the French and Polish, they built an electronic decoder which enabled them to read important German military communications between Hitler, Himmler, Goring, the general staff, and senior commanders. Unaware that its secret had been broken, the German high command continued to use Enigma (right) throughout the war. Messages were routinely deciphered and evaluated by intelligence officers working at Bletchley Park, about 50 miles outside London. Condensed versions of the communications (marked "Ultra Secret") were sent to top Allied commanders, enabling them to anticipate German movements and building their confidence in Allied strategy. The German intelligence breakdown became the Allies' best kept secret—unrevealed for nearly thirty years, until the mid-1970s.

reason I am saying this is that it seems like we get this spate of books, and you would almost infer from the books that they won the war with Ultra.

Quesada: I would say it was minimal.

Momyer: Particularly referring to the Battle of Britain, I think your assessment is probably closer to the truth. It really didn't have that fundamental an impact. It acted as a little bit better confirmation of what your other intelligence activities were telling you. But in terms of really changing how you employed the air, I can't see much evidence of it.

Lee: From my experience—and I had access to the information daily—I would say it had very little influence on air superiority. That was your question in the first place. Primarily most of the information I saw concerned the enemy ground forces, in rather large groups as a matter of fact.

Quesada: It had some information: the effect of air power on the ground forces.

Momyer: But didn't you get the kind of information that they had moved a group from this airfield to that airfield due to the instructions that were being issued? Therefore, this would set up an attack against that airfield based on the intercepted information and the breaking of the codes?

Lee: We had them covered anyway. That's why I said very little impact on air superiority.

Quesada: Spike, I think your question has to be answered another way. If those who received Ultra learned through it that certain airfields were being occupied and those airfields were attacked in the next day or so, whoever attacked them would go home. You could not use. . . .

Momyer: It was a tipoff that you had broken the code and, therefore, you really knew what was coming.

Quesada: You compromised the system. But I don't want to minimize the effect of instilling confidence. Confidence is a big factor in war. It was quite evident that the Germans were losing. Looking at it in retrospect, I think that until the end of the war, we didn't know how weak Germany really was. We failed, really, to recognize how weak they were.

Momyer: You know, though, there is one historical example where we used Ultra information. That was on Palm Sunday in 1943 in the shootdown of all those transports that were coming into North Africa, and I was up on that mission that. . . .[45]

Quesada: You got twelve, didn't you?

Momyer: Me?

Quesada: Yes. He shot down twelve airplanes that day.

Momyer: Not by a long shot.

Quesada: Now come on, how many?

Momyer: I didn't shoot any airplanes down there. I shot down Stukas, Ju–87s. It was in the El Guettar valley. That was another operation. And it was four. The mission that we ran that day, Palm Sunday, we really decimated that Ju–52 force. They were spread all along the coastline—we knew they were coming. At least the planning that was given to my group was about forty-eight hours in advance. We had a group of P–40s up for low-altitude coverage, and then we had an intermediate cover of Spitfires and then another high-altitude coverage of Spitfires. We were prepositioned on the basis of the exact time schedule that they were coming. We knew precisely when they were going to make the coast. We knew exactly what altitude they were flying. I think this is a specific example of information that really had an impact. I don't know of any other real example, except out in the Pacific where—who was it that was shot down?

Lee: Yamamoto.[46]

---

[45]On April 18, 1943 (Palm Sunday) in Tunisia, North Africa, four squadrons of American P–40s attacked a German Air Force transport convoy of approximately one hundred aircraft (Ju–52s). The Germans admitted to losing fifty-one transports, while the Americans claimed to have downed between fifty and seventy aircraft. See Wesley F. Craven and James L. Cate, eds, *The Army Air Forces in World War II*, 7 vols (Chicago, 1948–58), Vol II: *Europe: Torch to Pointblank, August 1942 to December 1943*, 191.

[46]Adm. Isoroku Yamamoto, commander in chief of the Japanese fleet, was killed by American

Momyer: I don't know of any other example from an air point of view that specific missions were tailored against that kind of information, except in the Battle of Britain.

Quesada: Neither do I.

The Late 1940s

Kohn: Coming out of World War II, the history books seem to emphasize so strongly the strategic use of air power. You will remember back into the late 1940s, the emphasis on—with the atomic bomb and with the development of new bomber fleets—nuclear and strategic air warfare. Several of you gentlemen were involved in tactical air forces; General Quesada was the first commander of TAC. Where did tactical air, and how did air superiority, fit in, in the late 1940s? Did our emphasis on strategic and nuclear air power do us harm? Did it diminish our ability in the area of air superiority? Did we forget air superiority after World War II, in that three- to five-year period?

Quesada: I don't claim any strong feelings or strong knowledge of that. I think, if I may speak in a philosophical way—and I think the rest of them here will have a better view of that than I—that the advent of the nuclear weapon resulted in a greater emphasis being put on strategic warfare and a lesser emphasis on tactical warfare. That was the result that I seem to remember. The others here will know better.

Lee: I will support that one hundred percent, because you and I both know. I was General Quesada's first chief of staff, incidentally, and then after a short period, his vice commander. The emphasis on strategic primarily had an impact on equipment and forces rather than doctrine. We kept that doctrine up. General Momyer will expound on it a little more because he was our plans and doctrine fellow. I think although we didn't have much capability to exercise our tactical doctrine, we still maintained

---

P–38 fighters which attacked his bomber and six escorting Zero fighters at Rabaul, New Britain, in the southwest Pacific on April 18, 1943. Yamamoto's itinerary had been detected by Ultra intelligence and relayed to U.S. Adm. Chester W. Nimitz. Nimitz questioned the wisdom of assassinating an opposing admiral and then, once he decided to order the attack, cleared his decision with Secretary of the Navy Frank Knox and President Franklin D. Roosevelt before proceeding. See E. B. Potter, *Nimitz* (Annapolis, Md., 1976), pp 233–34; Ronald Lewin, *The American Magic: Codes, Ciphers, and the Defeat of Japan* (New York, 1982), pp 186–191.

the philosophy of a requirement for control of the air in order to get proper tactical air operations. As a matter of fact, I think tactical air was just about, in the combat air forces, low man on the totem pole. Although we didn't have much air defense, at the same time tac air was going down in forces and equipment. The air defense force was building up command and control and a defense system, which turned into our SAGE [semiautomatic ground environment] system and things like that, but very little progress was being made in equipment. We were struggling with what we had left over, you might say, from World War II.[47]

Momyer: I think it was a struggle following World War II in which, as you well know, we were coming down to the forty-eight-group Air Force. Out of that forty-eight-group Air Force, there were some people advocating that tactical forces would have been a total of about six to eight groups. I think there was a basic difference of opinion philosophically within the Air Force, at that time. With the advent of the atomic bomb, a lot of people felt there would no longer be protracted war per se, that the magnitude of the weapon, the employment of the weapon, would be such that war would come to a conclusion one way or another in a relatively short period of time. During that early period, there was very little consideration as such, I think, for the employment of nuclear weapons on the battlefield. That came later for the simple reason that at that time, the technology prevented packaging a nuclear weapon into smaller components. People refer to the ''Fat Boy,''[48] a very large weapon and a relatively large yield.

I think the philosophical split with us in the tactical forces was that we weren't willing to concede that there wouldn't be wars other than just nuclear wars. I think that was the point. The other elements within the Air Force were convinced that conventional war was almost passé. Maybe that's a little extreme view, but I think it represented the philosophical split.

---

[47]Interview (K239.0512–729), Thomas A. Sturm, Office of Air Force History, and Hugh N. Ahmann, Albert F. Simpson Historical Research Center, with Gen. Earle E. Partridge, USAF, Retired, Colorado Springs, Colorado, April 23–25, 1974. Partridge was commander in chief of the Continental Air Defense Command from 1955 to his retirement in 1959.

[48]''Fat Boy'' or ''Fat Man'' was the colloquial term given to one of the two types of atomic bombs developed by engineers during the Manhattan Project. One bomb type used uranium and was detonated through a gun fuze device. The other type contained plutonium and was detonated with an implosive reaction. The former took the name ''Little Boy,'' and it devastated Hiroshima, Japan, on August 6, 1945. The latter, Fat Boy, destroyed Nagasaki, Japan, August 9, 1945. [Richard G. Hewlett and Oscar E. Anderson, Jr., *A History of the United States Atomic Energy Commission,* Vol I: *The New World, 1939–1946* (University Park Pa., 1962), 404–07.] For a history of how atomic weapons influenced the postwar Air Force, see Harry R. Borowski, *A Hollow Threat: Strategic Air Power and Containment Before Korea* (Westport, Conn., 1982).

Momyer as a colonel.

I think, as a result of that philosophical split, the tactical forces were put at a low level. I think the amplification of that, or the personification of that, was the fact that when General Quesada left TAC and General Lee took over they were putting the Tactical Air Command under the Continental Air Command. If anything, it reflected the basic philosophical split within the Air Force on how people looked at future war. In essence the two functions that you really got down to were these: one was the prosecution of the strategic offensive against the enemy, and the other was the denial of his offensive against you. You needed an air defense force, but you didn't really foresee a traditional air-ground campaign.

Ferguson: You didn't mention the procurement of aircraft during that period. It tells the story very clearly.

Momyer: I think it was reflected in the procurement of the aircraft, reflected in the amount of funds that went into it, and reflected in the whole allocation of resources. I agree with General Lee—I would have to for self-preservation—that our doctrine was alive and vigorous. As far as the tactical air was concerned, we were hammering those three priorities. All of our negotiations and discussions with the ground forces and the things that we tried to put in the maneuvers were all hammered against that experience.

I don't want to get into this, but it was further translated into the manuals that were written at the Air University, as I explained here some weeks ago, in the development of Air Force Manual 1–1. The job that I had in terms of preparing the basic doctrinal publications that the Air Force would come out with was the expression of these things. We have been talking about them this morning—theater air operations in which there was a manual on counterair. We got a little bit more sophisticated and called it air superiority. We called it counterair and then interdiction, close air support, reconnaissance, and airlift. So the doctrine was alive. I think the doctrine was vigorous. I don't think there was a lapse in doctrine between the conclusion of World War II and the onset of the Korean War. As General Ferguson just said, the reflection was in the equipment, the availability of equipment. There were other reflections; for example, our tactical control system had shrunk, the number of people that we had in the numbered air forces had shrunk, and the kind of equipment that we wanted to develop— the resources were not available. I think that kind of describes the perspective at the onset of the Korean War. I think our doctrine in that period of time was still alive, still being animated, still being articulated, and the reception, I would say, in the Air Staff was primarily more concerned with the strategic and the development of nuclear doctrine and the emphasis that was being devoted to it.

Quesada: As an example of the effect of the nuclear weapon, in terms of this discussion, was the effect it had on emphasizing strategic and minimizing tactical. There was a feeling on the part of some and a movement on the part of some to let the Army have the tactical air forces. For those who want to delve into the records, that is clear. There were some people in the Air Force who were pursuing the philosophy: "Let the Army have the tactical air forces." The reasoning was that the budget would be divided in three; let them bear the expense and we would have more money to put on strategic. One of the exponents of this, strange as it seems—and I hope I am not maligning him—was a fellow called "Freddy" Smith.[49] Do you remember that, Bob?

Lee: Yes.

---

[49]Gen. Frederic H. Smith, Jr. (1908–80) was Vice Chief of Staff, USAF, under Gen. Curtis E. LeMay from 1961 to 1962. A West Pointer, Smith rose to the rank of brigadier general in World War II. In the postwar years, Smith served as the chief of staff of the new Strategic Air Command established on March 21, 1946.

Quesada: There was a strong feeling among some, "Let them have the tactical air forces."

Kohn: There is a story that we agreed at the time of the debate over both unification and an independent air force, that if we became independent, we would never neglect the close air support mission. Did the Air Force make some kind of promise to the Army, in return for Army support for independence, after World War II? Is there any truth to that?

Quesada: Spaatz specifically said that in the strongest language to Eisenhower.

Kohn: Do you remember when at all, General Quesada? In what context....

Quesada: Eisenhower was Chief of Staff of the Army.[50] It was before he left as Chief of Staff of the Army. I wasn't there, but I was told about it in no uncertain terms by Spaatz. Spaatz told me that he had made the promise to Eisenhower. "And goddammit, don't let him down," he said. Spaatz made that specific promise to Eisenhower as a way of encouraging Eisenhower to lend support to the establishment of the United States Air Force.

Ferguson: I think you will find it in the testimony before the Vinson Committee, November 1947, when the final hearings over the decision were taken.[51] I think it is in there, because I happened to be sitting in at the hearings that day.

Quesada: I remember specifically that Spaatz gave me a strong admonition, in stronger language than he normally used, that he had made this promise and he didn't want to be let down by a half-assed implementation of it.

---

[50]General of the Army Dwight D. Eisenhower was Chief of Staff, U.S. Army, from November 1945 to June 1948. During these years, the Department of Defense came into existence amidst bitter disputes between the services over roles, missions, organizations, and budgets. A central issue was the mission of an independent air force and its component forces. Eisenhower supported establishing an independent air force.

[51]Hearings before the Committee on Expenditures in the Executive Departments, House of Representatives, April 2, 24, 25, 29; May 2, 6–8, 13, 15; June 10–12, 17–19, 20, 24, 26, 30; July 1, 1947, 78th Congress, 1st session (Washington, 1947), pp 294–300, 328–336; James E. Hewes, Jr., *From Root to McNamara: Army Organization and Administration, 1900–1963* (Washington, 1975), pp

Momyer: If you go back and really look at the record, it would seem that the Air Force was more interested in gaining the status of a separate air force than it was in unification. They were almost willing to make any kind of concession that would enhance the attainment of a separate air force. I think it is apropos to the debate that's going on now with regard to the proposal that Jones[52] has made about reorganizing the JCS [Joint Chiefs of Staff]. If you will look at the record, the Navy obviously was opposed and is opposed today to changing the JCS. They are opposed to any changes. On the other hand, the Army from the outset had proposed a single Chief of Staff with a General Staff. What you have got today in "Shy" Meyer's[53] proposal is just a little alteration of that basic proposal. On the other hand, the Air Force throughout all the unification hearings seemed to say, "Don't rock the boat boys as long as we get this separate Air Force."

Quesada: I assure you that was the philosophy of the time. I was there and a party to it.

The Korean War

Kohn: We talk now about air superiority doctrine being alive and well in the late 1940s. The promise was made to the Army to maintain the close air support mission. Yet the Air Force was oriented toward the strategic mission with its equipment, as General Ferguson has said, and its procurement. Along came Korea. You had the doctrine; you had the lessons learned; the forces were joined in June 1950. General Weyland[54] noted the

---

163–67. Verification of this discussion can be found in interview (K239.0512–838), Lt. Col. Steven W. Long, Jr., USAF, and Lt. Col. Ralph W. Stephenson, USAF, with Lt. Gen. Elwood R. Quesada, USAF, Retired, May 12–13, 1975.

[52]In February 1982 Gen. David C. Jones, USAF, Chairman, Joint Chiefs of Staff, proposed significant changes in the structure and responsibilities of the Joint Chiefs of Staff. Specifically, Jones suggested: (1) strengthening the role of the chairman, (2) expanding the training, experience, and rewards of joint duty. See Gen. David C. Jones, "Why the Joint Chiefs of Staff Must Change," *Armed Forces Journal*, 119 (March 1982), 62–72; *New York Times*, February 18, 25, and March 1, 5, 1982.

[53]Gen. Edward C. Meyer, Chief of Staff, U.S. Army, also testified before Congress concerning the reform of the Joint Chiefs of Staff. General Meyer advocated creating a stronger chairman and a more professional, trained joint staff which would serve the chairman. See Gen. Edward C. Meyer, "The JCS—How Much Reform is Needed?" *Armed Forces Journal*, 119 (April 1982), 82–90; *New York Times*, March 31, 1982.

[54]Gen. Otto P. Weyland (1902–79) was deputy commander of the National War College when the Korean War broke out in June 1950. Within a few weeks he went to the Far East Air Forces, the principal command waging the air war for Korea. Initially he was the Vice Commander for Operations, Far East Air Forces, but within a year he had risen to commander, leading the command through ten campaigns in Korea. After the war, General Weyland stayed in the Far East and assisted the Japanese in reorganizing and reequipping their air forces. See Robert F. Futrell, *The United States Air Force in Korea, 1950–1953* (New York, 1961), pp 116–17, 199–201, 255, 441–47, 500–1.

constant struggle he had with each of the Army commanders in Korea, who did not want the Air Force commander to operate independently of the ground forces. Supposedly we had worked this out; we had the doctrine. Why has this been a recurring problem? It comes up in our discussion of roles and missions today and has been a constant theme of our military history, not just the last thirty years, but even long before that. How did that affect air superiority in the Korean war?

Momyer: Jim was right out there in the middle of that.

Lee: You made one statement that we had the doctrine. *We* had the doctrine, but the Army didn't have it. Furthermore, we might just mention a little bit that the Air Force doctrine was partly injected into the papers, Joint Action of the Armed Forces, in the late 1940s.[55]

Momyer: Known as JCS Pub 2 today.[56]

Lee: Anyway, I think Forrest Sherman[57] and Norstad[58] worked on these papers. They went as far as they could with some Army help. Then they sent these documents out for review and completion to various elements of the armed services. About five of them came down to Spike and me at TAC after you had left, Pete. We were to work these things out with the Navy and Marines over at Norfolk and the Army Field Forces at Fort Monroe, Virginia. We spent months on these things, meeting at the lowest staff level

---

[55]Joint Action of the Armed Forces Papers were published in manual form on September 19, 1951. These papers were coordinated statments on the roles and missions of the component parts of the Army and Air Force. The manual was superseded by JCS Publication 2, *Unified Action Armed Forces (UAAF)*, November 1, 1959, which codified in a joint publication the missions and command relationships of the armed services as legislated in the Department of Defense Reorganization Act of 1958.

[56]JCS Publication 2, *Unified Action Armed Forces (UNAAF)*, October 1974.

[57]Adm. Forrest P. Sherman, USN (1896–1951), became the Chief of Naval Operations in November 1949. A graduate of the Naval Academy, Sherman had a lengthy career in naval aviation before rising to command positions during World War II. In the postwar years Admiral Sherman represented the Navy in many of the arguments over unification and the creation of an independent Air Force. See Lawrence J. Korb, *The Joint Chiefs of Staff: The First Twenty-Five Years* (Bloomington, Ind., 1976), pp 56–57, 71, 67–68.

[58]Gen. Lauris Norstad, USAF (1907–). In 1949–50 Norstad, who had compiled a brilliant career in intelligence, planning, and operations during World War II, was at Headquarters USAF serving as the Deputy Chief of Staff for Operations. In October 1950 he went to Europe as the Commander in Chief, United States Air Forces in Europe. For the next thirteen years Norstad served in Europe in a series of Air Force, joint service, and NATO commands. For a personal interpretation of postwar negotiations for an independent Air Force, see Lauris Norstad, "The National Security Act of 1947: Implications and Interpretations," in *Evolution of the American Military Establishment Since World War II*, ed: Paul R. Schratz (Lexington, Va., 1978), pp 23–30.

and then finally meeting with General Devers[59] with my sitting across the table with our helpers. We got a lot accomplished in there, but there were certain items which we split right straight down the middle and sent back to Norstad and our side for them to try to resolve. They decided they didn't have time for this, so they formed specific elements, so-called, in which representatives of the two commands would meet. In our case it was TAC and Army Field Forces working—wasn't it—"air support of ground forces"?

Momyer: Yes. 31–35.[60]

Lee: Spike and I were Tactical Air Command people. We sat in the Pentagon with a fellow named Brooks[61] and Major General McClure[62] from the Army. We sat in the Pentagon up here for about two sessions of a five-day week trying to work these things out, and we made some progress. But there were some things on which we split down the middle and handed back to General Norstad on the Air Staff. I found that—several years later after I became Director of Plans, we would go down to meetings of the Joint Chiefs of Staff—those things still weren't resolved in 1952–53. It was 1949 when the specific elements finally turned our work back to our respective services. I don't know whether it is solved now or not. You know more about it than I do.

Momyer: I think, without any question, the Army accepted the fact that we had to have air superiority. But it was more or less just a statement. I think they had had reservations about the importance of interdiction. I don't think during that period of time the Army view changed, in spite of the fact that after the war Eisenhower held a meeting with all of his top commanders

---

[59]Gen. Jacob L. Devers, USA (1887–1979), commanded the 6th Army Group during World War II, consisting of the U.S. Seventh Army and the French First Army, and in August 1944 led this force into southern France. After the war he served as the Chief, Army Ground Forces, a position which placed him on a level with the Chief, Army Air Forces. In March 1948 General Eisenhower, Chief of Staff, U.S. Army, ordered a reorganization of the Army. Devers became Chief, Army Field Forces, and established his headquarters at Fort Monroe, Virginia.

[60]Immediately after World War II, General Arnold directed the Army Air Forces Board to prepare operational field service regulations which would reflect the proven air-ground doctrine accumulated from combat experience. The result was War Department Field Manual 31–35, *Air-Ground Operations,* August 13, 1946. This manual was coordinated throughout the War Department and with the Chief, Army Ground Forces, Gen. Jacob L. Devers.

[61]Lt. Gen. Edward H. Brooks, USA (1893–1978), commanded Army forces in the Caribbean.

[62]Maj. Gen. Robert B. McClure, USA (1896–1973), was Chief of Staff, Second Army, during these board meetings.

to review the lessons of World War II. What he did at that meeting was to confirm the same thing they had decided at Tripoli. Following the war, as the experience level started to drain away, the Army position kept coming back to wanting operational control of the aircraft that were engaged in close air support: the commander in contact with the troops had to have control of the forces that were engaged. That was one basis of the split that was developing. At the same time we had the continuing split with the Navy over control of naval air, which is the same argument that's going on today. As Jim will point out, it is the same argument that went on during the Korean War. I think what we see as we moved into Korea is a basic underlying split in spite of the experience that came out of World War II.

Quesada: Let me give you a little anecdote. Doctrine is awfully fine, but doctrine is nothing more than a whole group of words. A lot depends on the personality of the people who are implementing doctrine. Let me give you an example, and it involves some of the people who are here. Our effort in Vietnam—I was long retired, and I would read about it in the newspapers—to me as far as air power was concerned was a little bit of what I used to refer

Maj. Gen. Robert M. Lee.

69

to as operational masturbation. I have always felt the B–52s were to a large extent bombing forests. There was a lot of discontent in the services and certainly on the Hill about this. My personal friend, Stuart Symington,[63] who was then a Senator, arranged for me to go over to Vietnam. Who was the Chief of Staff then? McConnell.[64] It was with his full support.

Well, it was just clear to me that tactical air power as being exercised in that theater was the product of the Army and Army thinking. The guy who was in command of the air forces in that theater was selected because he was a friend of General Westmoreland's[65] and from his same hometown. They were brought up together. That isn't what you need. You need somebody who has conviction and also a personality and enough arrogance—if you don't mind my calling it that—to stand up. When I came back— there were some other things that occurred—but when I came back, I recommended very strongly that the guy who was there in command of the air forces was selected for the wrong reason. He was selected because he was a friend of Westmoreland's and would get along. You need somebody there who understands the use of air power and doesn't give a goddamn about getting along. I suggested Spike Momyer.

Momyer: The perfect choice. [Laughter.]

Quesada: You remember that, don't you, Spike?

Momyer: The perfect choice for any commander.

Quesada: Isn't that true.

---

[63]Stuart Symington (1901–) was Secretary of the Air Force from 1947 to 1950. During the campaign for an independent air force (1946–47), Symington served as Assistant Secretary of War for Air, January 1946–September 1947. He vigorously supported the reorganization of the War and Navy Departments into a three-service, unified Department of Defense and helped persuade Congress to support this change. In the late 1940s Symington advocated a 70–group Air Force and a national policy of strategic nuclear deterrence. Resigning in 1950 from his position as Secretary of the Air Force, Symington held key positions in the Truman administration before running for the U.S. Senate from Missouri in 1953. He served in the Senate from 1952 to 1976, prior to his retirement. [Eleanora W. Schoenebaum, ed, *The Truman Years,* Political Profiles Series (New York, 1978), pp 527–29.]

[64]Gen. John P. McConnell (1908–), was the Air Force chief of staff from February 1965 to July 1969. These years constituted the period of the largest commitment of U.S. forces to the war in Vietnam.

[65]Gen. William C. Westmoreland, USA (1914–), commanded the Military Assistance Command, Vietnam (MACV). For Westmoreland's account of the war, see Gen. William C. Westmoreland, USA, Ret, *A Soldier Reports* (Garden City, N.Y., 1976).

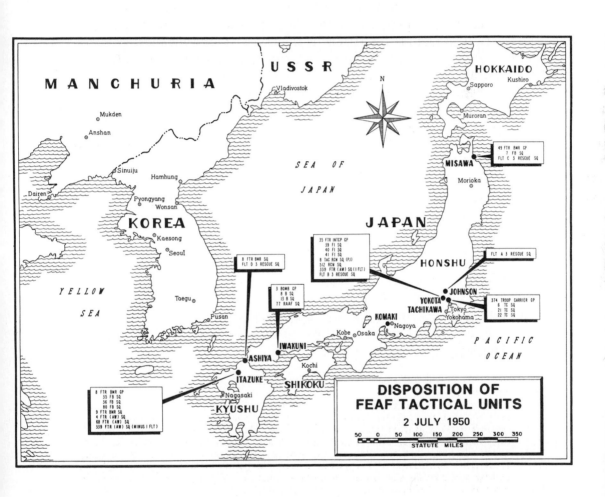

MANCHURIA

USSR

HOKKAIDO

Sapporo
Kushiro

Vladivostok

Mukden

Anshan

Muroran

SEA OF

JAPAN

49 FTR BMR GP
7 FB SQ
FLT C 3 RESCUE SQ

MISAWA

Sinuiju

Hamhung

Dairen

Pyongyang
Wonsan

Morioka

KOREA

Kaesong

Seoul

JAPAN

35 FTR INTCP GP
39 FI SQ
40 FI SQ
41 FI SQ
8 TAC RCN SQ (PJ)
512 RCN SQ
339 FTR (AW) SQ (1 FLT)
FLT B 3 RESCUE SQ

HONSHU

FLT A 3 RESCUE SQ

8 FTR BMR SQ
FLT D 3 RESCUE SQ

YELLOW

Taegu

JOHNSON

SEA

YOKOTA
TACHIKAWA

374 TROOP CARRIER GP
6 TC SQ
21 TC SQ
22 TC SQ

3 BOMB GP
8 B SQ
13 B SQ
77 RAAF SQ

Tokyo

Pusan

KOMAKI

Yokohama

Kobe
Osaka

Nagoya

PACIFIC

IWAKUNI

OCEAN

ASHIYA

Kochi

ITAZUKE

SHIKOKU

8 FTR BMR GP
35 FB SQ
36 FB SQ
80 FB SQ
9 FTR BMR SQ
4 FTR (AW) SQ
68 FTR (AW) SQ
339 FTR (AW) SQ (MINUS 1 FLT)

Nagasaki

KYUSHU

**DISPOSITION OF
FEAF TACTICAL UNITS**

2 JULY 1950

50   0   50 100 150 200 250 300 350
STATUTE MILES

B-29 Superfortresses on the way to attack Anju, an important supply and communications center serving North Korean forces.

Momyer: Oh, yes. We are kind of deviating here, but I didn't know that you had been out there prior to my assignment and you had come back and made some recommendations with regard to the command organization. I went out ahead of assignment. I went out really in April, and I wasn't due for assignment until June. I came back, and McConnell said, "What do you think?" I ran down what I thought was the necessary reorganization that had to take place and what had to be done in terms of air. He said, "You must have been talking to Pete Quesada." My recommendations were almost identical with the observations that you had made.

Quesada: I want to make sure that my point is taken and not the personalities involved. You can have all the doctrine you want, but unless you have people, commanders, to implement those doctrines, you might as well throw your doctrines away.

Momyer: What were your observations in Korea, Jim, with regard to these....

Ferguson: We were talking about doctrine. I arrived in Japan about ten days after the outbreak of hostilities to serve as special assistant to Gen. O. P. Weyland. Having served with "Opie" in Europe, we lost no time in getting to the heart of the problem. The Eighth Army headquarters in Korea and MacArthur's headquarters in Tokyo were composed mostly of people whose experience was in the Pacific. Few if any were familiar with, or had experience in, the closely coordinated air and ground actions as they were conducted in Europe. There was also a general reluctance to adopt procedures other than those employed across the many Pacific islands. To correct this, someone, with tongue in cheek, suggested an airdrop over

72

Eighth Army headquarters consisting of a load of Manual 31–35s, which describes the operation of the air-ground team. There was reluctance on the part of MacArthur's staff to adopt the European doctrine, but persuasion on the part of "Pat" Partridge and "Opie" Weyland brought them around, partly.[66]

The Navy and Marines were a different story. With the introduction of the Marine division into the Eighth Army front came the Marine air division [1st Marine Aircraft Wing]. Because of the aircraft limitations—as well as their doctrine—this wing was confined exclusively to close support of its Marine division. A Marine liaison officer was planned in our joint operations center to coordinate their activities. I should mention also that, in addition to the U.S. and Korean divisions, we had a [United Nations] division and also a South African Air Force fighter squadron. All these elements came under the Eighth Army and Fifth Air Force with the air-ground coordination taking place at the Fifth Air Force joint operations center. In summary, we maintained the World War II proven concept of keeping enemy air off the backs of the ground forces, cut up the lines of supply, and furnished close support where and when needed.

Kohn: In a situation like this, in the initial stage of an enemy offensive, must air superiority take a backseat to close air support and air interdiction, and must you constantly be balancing the priorities with your air forces?

Ferguson: Yes, you must balance priorities, yet there is no set piece. When war breaks out, as in the case of Korea, the geography, the opposition, and the resources available to you set the plan of action. Basically, establishing air superiority takes priority if one has the resources. In the case of Korea, in the early stages of the action around Taegu, there was very little enemy air action. Our first priority was to help stabilize the ground situation by interdicting the supply routes. Where friendly forces were in danger of being overrun, close support was concentrated in that area. You

---

[66]Gen. Otto P. Weyland (see note 53) and Gen. Earle E. "Pat" Partridge (1900–). Partridge was a major general commanding the Fifth Air Force in Japan when the North Koreans invaded the south in June 1950. Specifically, on June 25 when the North Korean armies moved into South Korea, he responded by directing his air forces to fly to the Korean peninsula and begin evacuating Americans. While the war progressed Partridge remained in the Far East, becoming in April 1951 commander of the Far East Air Forces. This stint as commander was brief, lasting just seven weeks, Lt. Gen. Otto P. Weyland being named commander in early June 1951. Then a lieutenant general, Partridge returned to the United States for two years before going back to the Far East, this time as a four-star general commanding the Far East Air Forces (1954–55).

will recall that when the necessary forces were assembled, heavy air attacks assisted a breakout of the Taegu perimeter,[67] and there was a rapid advance north. The Chinese counterattack then changed the picture as our forces withdrew to the 38th parallel where the ground action stabilized. During the rapid advance and later withdrawal, we saw little or no enemy air; our first priority was protection of our supply lines and close support. With the ground action stabilized, enemy air activity picked up, airfields were being rebuilt, and an air threat appeared to be developing. Action now was to destroy airfields in North Korea using B–29s escorted by F–86s. Once we selected targets near the Yalu River, enemy air became very active and the air war became the primary form of action. To summarize, the centralized control of the air permits shifting from hour to hour to targets of highest priority and greatest contribution to the success of the operation.

Momyer: I think one of the things that comes out of the Korean War— unfortunately it's a terrible thing to say, but I feel we would be in a much stronger position today with regard to the importance of air superiority if the enemy had been able to penetrate and bomb some of our airfields and had been able to bomb the frontlines periodically. It would have brought home to our ground forces and other people the importance of air superiority. The fact is that most of our air forces came out of World War II never having experienced a condition in which they had to operate without air superiority. In the Korean War there wasn't a single attack that I have been able to identify that was put against our ground forces. So air superiority has remained almost a philosophical thing. The Army has never had to operate in an environment where it had to consider: "Do we dare make this move at 12 o'clock noon because that road is under the surveillance of enemy aircraft, or can we move that division from here to here during this period of time, and what kind of condition is it going to be in, or can we launch this attack in the period of time that we think is essential?" Those considerations are absent in all of the planning by virtue of this experience; they have never had to fight without air superiority. The reason that air superiority was so far removed from the Eighth Army is that Weyland and you people were up there containing them along the Yalu and Weyland and you were keeping those airfields knocked out so that the enemy couldn't deploy within range of the Eighth Army. So air superiority became so far

---

[67]Also known as the Pusan perimeter.

removed from the thinking and the activities of the Army that it was more concerned with close air support, and that became the primary emphasis.

Ferguson: We had sufficient freedom of activity up to the Yalu River that we could monitor on a day-to-day basis the construction or reconstruction of airfields, and when they got to a length of three thousand feet, off went a B–29 or two and "postholed" the repairs. Then it was out of commission for six weeks or two months. In retrospect it's worth just one word to go back to the end of World War II. The Luftwaffe did have one last gasp. On the first of January 1945. Do you remember that? New Year's Day, early in the morning. So we did lose quite a few airplanes on that one.[68]

Quesada: If you had been alert, you wouldn't have.

Ferguson: Well, it was New Year's morning, yet our strikes were on their way to their targets. What we lost were spares.

Quesada: Well, we didn't lose any. We shot them down.

Ferguson: That's right, you did, some of them.

Quesada: We flew the—incidentally, what was that guy's name who became Vice Chief of Staff who was an ace from the Eighth Air Force?

Momyer: J. C. Meyer.[69]

---

[68]This air battle occurred during the Battle of the Bulge, December 16, 1944, to January 31, 1945. In the battle the Germans counterattacked in the thick forest of the Ardennes, throwing the Allies back. The Germans projected that, if successful, they would be able to envelop the U.S. First and Ninth Armies and the British 21st Army Group, thus destroying twenty to thirty Allied divisions. On January 1, 1945, the German Air Force attacked Allied air bases in the Netherlands, Belgium, and France. Between eight and ten in the morning, approximately 700 German aircraft destroyed 156 Allied aircraft. [Wesley F. Craven and James L. Cate, eds, *The Army Air Forces in World War II*, 7 vols (Chicago, 1948–58), Vol III: *Europe: Argument to V–E Day, January 1944 to May 1945*, 665–66, 701–3.]

[69]Gen. John C. Meyer (1919–75) arrived in the European theater in January 1943 in command of the 487th Fighter Squadron, Eighth Air Force. Meyer flew two hundred combat missions and personally shot down twenty-four German aircraft and is credited with destroying another 13.5 aircraft on the ground. This combat record made Meyer one of the leading U.S. aces of World War II. A lieutenant colonel at the end of the war, Meyer stayed in the Air Force, serving in Korea where he flew F–86 Sabre jets against Mig–15s, destroying two enemy jets. Later, General Meyer served as the Air Force vice chief of staff (1969–72) and as the commander in chief of Strategic Air Command (1972–74). For Meyer's war record see Edward H. Sims, *American Aces in Great Fighter Battles of World War II* (New York, 1958).

Quesada: They attacked one of their groups at Maastricht [Netherlands]. He shot an airplane down before he got his wheels up. We were alert enough, as you all weren't, and saw they were going to do it, and we put pilots in every light flak position around the airport for two weeks to be there a half hour before dawn.

Kohn: Let us go back to Korea for a moment. Even though the Army didn't understand the air superiority question, you—facing enemy air forces up at the Yalu—must have been concerned about air superiority. Yet, you weren't allowed to attack the enemy's air force at its source.

Ferguson: Not across the river.

Kohn: Not across the river, which, of course, must have been basic to the doctrine coming out of World War II. Did these rules of engagement bother you at the time?

Ferguson: This was not a question of doctrine. Higher authority directed that our operations be limited to the geographical limits of North Korea. Thus, although our B–29s and fighters came within a few miles of Mig bases across the Yalu, we were denied the opportunity of wiping them out on the ground and thus improving the protection of the B–29s.

Momyer: Don't you think, though, if you would have been confronted with a hard decision, if those Migs had begun to come south where they would challenge your whole posture, your airfields and so forth—but you didn't have that. I think one of the reasons is that the preponderance of those aircraft along the Yalu were Soviet, flown by Soviet pilots. People forget that.

Ferguson: I think if Migs had appeared anywhere near the 38th parallel, the story could have been quite different.

Momyer: They keep talking about the Chinese pilots up there and a great number of Koreans, but the Soviets were rotating a new squadron in every six weeks, and they weren't anxious to get them down south.

Ferguson: You are right, I am sure; the Soviets weren't anxious to expose their participation.

Momyer: They controlled them up there. They would get a squadron of pilots indoctrinated, and you could see that by the tactics that were used, for example, with a new outfit that would come in. A pilot would stay up at the higher altitudes and reluctantly come down. If you looked at the pattern, as he would come toward the end of his training period, he would get more aggressive. So you had a self-limitation on the part of that air force. On the other hand, and I think this was political, the Soviets didn't want to overtly get engaged.

So we had an artificial condition that led to that containment of air superiority along the Yalu. But it could have been entirely different. A political decision would have had to have been made about those sanctuaries if there had been that amount of effort put against Fifth Air Force and put against the Eighth Army. It would have had to be reconsidered.

The same way, I think, as in the Vietnam War. If suddenly the Soviet air forces had started to appear in Vietnam operating out of sanctuaries in China and had really begun to bring us under attack, we would have been confronted with a tremendous political decision as to whether those bases were going to be denied. Otherwise, we would have had to quit operating up north. You just couldn't have done it in that kind of an operation.

Ferguson: Further to the tactical war and the support of the Army: as you know, at the beginning of the Korean War, P–80s had just appeared on the scene in an air defense configuration. The rest of the airplanes were P–51s, and I think one group of F–84s had arrived about that time.

Quesada: –84s or –86s?

Ferguson: F–84s arrived shortly after the outbreak, and F–86s later. The F–80s were quickly modified to carry larger fuel tanks, and bomb racks were added to the wings. Our tactical control group radars were quickly modified to control bombers on night attack—a further development of a technique we used late in World War II. Close radar control permitted area bombing of targets at night and in bad weather. By knowing the location of the target—usually a troop concentration—and the precise position of the bomber relative to the target, quite good accuracy could be obtained.

Momyer: Jim, how about expanding a little bit on the relationship with naval air and the control of the air along the Yalu.

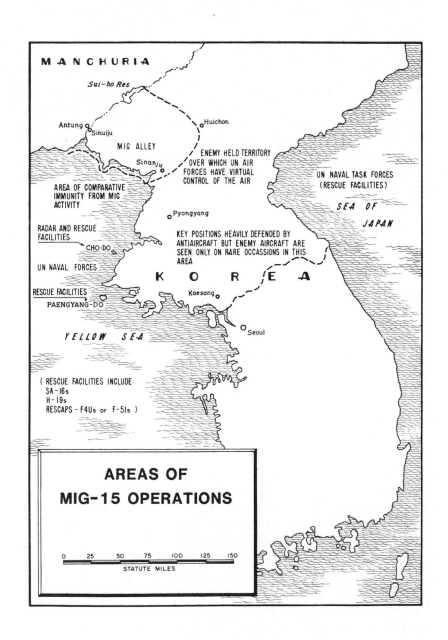

MANCHURIA

Sui-ho Res.

Antung

Sinuiju

Huichon

MIG ALLEY

Sinanju

ENEMY HELD TERRITORY
OVER WHICH UN AIR
FORCES HAVE VIRTUAL
CONTROL OF THE AIR

UN NAVAL TASK FORCES
(RESCUE FACILITIES)

AREA OF COMPARATIVE
IMMUNITY FROM MIG
ACTIVITY

SEA OF
JAPAN

Pyongyang

RADAR AND RESCUE
FACILITIES

CHO-DO

KEY POSITIONS HEAVILY DEFENDED BY
ANTIAIRCRAFT BUT ENEMY AIRCRAFT ARE
SEEN ONLY ON RARE OCCASSIONS IN THIS
AREA

UN NAVAL FORCES

K O R E A

RESCUE FACILITIES

PAENGYANG-DO

Kaesong

Seoul

YELLOW SEA

(RESCUE FACILITIES INCLUDE:
SA-16s
H-19s
RESCAPS-F4Us or F-51s)

AREAS OF
MIG-15 OPERATIONS

0   25   50   75   100   125   150

STATUTE MILES

Heavily loaded F-84 Thunderjets (above) wing their way through Korean skies, headed for enemy targets.

Soviet-built Mig-15.

Far East Air Forces Commanding General, Lt. Gen. George E. Stratemeyer (pointing), confers with his principal staff officers at FEAF Headquarters in Japan. Standing (l. to r.) are Brig. Gen. James E. Ferguson, Assistant Deputy for Operations; Maj. Gen. Laurence C. Craigie, Vice Commander; and Brig. Gen. Darr H. Alkire, Deputy for Materiel. Seated are (l. to r.) Brig. Gen. Jarred V. Crabb, Deputy for Operations; Brig. Gen. Oliver S. Picher, Deputy for Personnel; and Brig. Gen. William P. Nuckols, Public Information Officer.

High-performance F-86 Sabre jets were essential in maintaining American air superiority in Korea. Here, aircraft of the 51st Fighter-Interceptor Wing streak toward "Mig Alley" in northwest Korea to look for enemy Mig-15s, October 1952.

USAF's first jet aircraft in Korea, F-80 Shooting Star, heads for a North Korean target to dump its twin tanks of napalm.

Ferguson: Earlier, I mentioned the introduction of the Marine air wing to support its infantry division. We worked out a satisfactory integration of the air and ground action along the front. Naval air was another matter. Here, not only doctrine but command prerogatives, aircraft limitations, and communications difficulties created a situation difficult to reconcile. The aircraft aboard the carriers had limited performance versus Mig–15s, and radius of action depended greatly upon the position of the carrier task force. Furthermore, communication to and from the carrier task force to the joint operations center in Seoul were very unreliable. It was, therefore, decided to designate the northeastern portion of North Korea as the area over which carrier aircraft could operate, electing, for the most part, their own targets.

Momyer: The eastern portion up near Wonchon.

Ferguson: Yes, that's right.

Momyer: I guess the thing I was really trying to draw out, one of the things that is in the records—and it gets back to the performance of aircraft, the importance of air superiority—is that to be able to survive in the environment the weapon system must be tailored so that it can fight in the environment. The Navy asked to be withdrawn from patrols along the Yalu because the performance of their aircraft was such they couldn't compete with the Mig–15 and the Mig–17. It had to be handled by the F–86s. I think this drives home the point that if you are going to be able to control the air, you have got to have the performance in the weapon systems to be able to survive in the environment. If the F–86 had had the kind of low performance the Navy aircraft had, we wouldn't have been able to contain the Migs along the Yalu.

Ferguson: Yes. I mentioned that both Marine and Navy aircraft had performance limitations which limited their employment.

Momyer: We really had three elements of the problem as far as naval aviation was concerned. One was the lack of performance to be able to carry on the air superiority battle. Secondly, the command and control argument that there ought to be a single air commander, and a single air commander then assigns out the task for the employment of naval aviation. Then finally, the control of Marine aviation, when Marine aviation is engaged in less than an amphibious operation, should come under the command and control of the air component commander. Don't you think those are about the three things?

Ferguson: Yes, of course. But command and control was the most difficult problem to resolve. With the Marine division sandwiched in between U.S. and Korean divisions along the front, as I remember, and dedicated air with limited range and performance, the only solution was a compromise. A liaison officer from the Marine air wing served in the Fifth Air Force joint operations center to coordinate their activities within the Fifth Air Force.

Momyer: It has been brought out in arguments with regards to the control of Marine air with the X Corps. General Almond was the X Corps commander. After the Inchon invasion he wanted to retain control of the 1st Marine Air Wing, and the X Corps would operate actually independent of the Eighth Army.[70] This led to the question then of control of the air under a single air component.

---

[70]In mid–September 1950 General of the Army Douglas MacArthur counterattacked with a bold amphibious assault at Inchon near the capital city of Seoul. Maj. Gen. Edward M. Almond, USA, commanded the landing force consisting of the U.S. Army X Corps, including the U.S. Marine 1st Division. During the planning phases, Marine staff officers convinced General Almond to place all Marine tactical air forces under the operational control of the corps commander. General Almond and Brig. Gen. Thomas J. Cushman, USMC, would have direct command over the assets of the Marine tactical air forces over the invasion area. This organizational arrangement, authorized by General

Kohn: Was there a heavy percentage of lessons learned in World War II that had to be relearned in Korea? As I am hearing you speak, I am sensing that the Navy and the Marines and the Army had to relearn the lessons of World War II. The Air Force understood those lessons and simply had to reeducate the other services. Am I overstating that, perhaps?

Ferguson: General Almond, who had come from MacArthur's staff, tried hard to retain the Marine Air Wing as an element of his corps. Communications with his headquarters were extremely difficult, suggesting more than technical difficulties. It's too bad that so much effort is expended in getting the same side to work together. I suppose it will always be thus.

Quesada: And it will in the next conflict, too.

Momyer: I don't think the Marine air doctrine changed from World War II to Korea to the present. In the current arguments of the so-called self-containment of the MAGTAF [Marine Air-Ground Task Force] as a separate component of the service, it seems to me that the fundamental position hasn't changed. I think with respect to the control of naval aviation, the same view and arguments have prevailed in World War II, and the same arguments have prevailed in Korea and again in Vietnam. I can't see that there have been any significant changes in those basic positions.

Kohn: Could we shift for a moment to the question of the aircraft in air superiority in the Korean War: the lopsided scores in the dogfights between the F–86s and the Mig–15s? Do you think air superiority depends more on the quality of the aircraft than on the quantity?

Momyer: We are into the old argument of high-low mix again. Some people take extreme positions. I will say, from my own experience, there is no question that you have got to have quality, but you have got to have a balance with quantity, or you will simply go out of business through

---

MacArthur, ran counter to the established air coordination agreement between the Army and the Air Force which made the senior Air Force general the coordinator of air operations in the Korean theater. [Robert F. Futrell, *The United States Air Force in Korea, 1950–1953* (New York, 1961), pp 144–45; Historical Branch, USMC, *United States Marine Operations in Korea, 1950–1953*, 5 vols (Washington, 1954–72), Vol II: *The Inchon-Seoul Operation*, by Lynn Montross and Nicholas A. Canzona, 70–71.]

attrition. So there is a proper balance. I happen to believe—and I am on this side of the argument—I emphasize quality rather than quantity. In other words if I have to make a choice, then I will go with the quality side of the argument. I think in the situation where I have a numerically inferior force, but I have a qualitatively superior force, I have a better opportunity to translate that into an advantage than I have vice versa. As long as I have qualitative inferiority, I have really released to the opposing enemy air force the initiative. To me that's the most important thing. As long as I have the qualitative superiority, then I still have the option of the initiative. If I have the option of the initiative, I can select where I want to engage and how I want to engage and when I want to disengage. I can't do that with a qualitative inferiority.

Ferguson: I think, also, the training of the crews has a bearing on it, and I think our F–86 people were considerably better qualified and more aggressive than the people they ran up against.

Kohn: We want to ask you about the experience level of these crews, also. Sixty-eight percent of the pilots who destroyed Migs were over twenty-eight years old and had flown an average of eighteen missions in World War II. Do you think that was a critical factor in the air-to-air struggle?

Ferguson: I think it was a very important one, yes. Experience and probably a higher level of training, even without World War II experience, than what they ran up against. Confidence in their equipment. It was a fine performing airplane with no aerodynamic limitations; on the other side pilots had to be quite careful.

Momyer: I think that would be an interesting comparison: what the average age was of the people that did sixty to seventy percent of shooting down of the aircraft in World War II as compared to Korea. I think you would find the age was around twenty-two rather than up at this higher level. I think one of the reasons is that in World War II we were bringing in pilots in droves. We were expanding, and we had just a very limited number of people that had any years of service. For example, ninety-nine percent of our groups were made up of Reserve officers. So we had a very limited amount of experience. On the other hand, we didn't call back any significant numbers of people as far as the Korean War was concerned. So what we sent over were the hardcore professionals that had this added number of years. I think that accounts probably more for the number who were older, who did the shooting down of the aircraft, rather than it being a function of age. They were people with experience. I think that accounts more for it than whether those twenty-eight-year-olds were more competent than the twenty-two-year-olds of World War II.

Kohn: Could I ask you all a question of speculation about the enemy in the Korean War? Do you think there was a lack of knowledge of air warfare on the part of the enemy in Korea that prevented them from making the most of their airpower capabilities?

Ferguson: I think we have already mentioned the fact that there were other than North Koreans involved there. If you could look at it from a Russian point of view, it was really an advanced training operation. They thought of it in quite a different way than we did. We were trying to solve the whole Korean question and drive the enemy out of North Korea, or certainly subdue them at the 38th parallel, which had been an agreed-to position at the end of World War II. So our objective and theirs appeared to be dissimilar.

Kohn: So air superiority in effect was not an issue for them.

Momyer: I don't think there was any doctrine in the North Korean Air Force nor any significant doctrine in the Chinese so-called forces with regards to air operations at all at that particular time. You are really talking about the Soviet Union, and I think the Soviet Union's political restraints that we are talking about and that General Ferguson has pointed out made it a training ground. That was an optimum training ground for them along the Yalu.

The General Problem of Air Superiority

Kohn: Could I raise a general question that can be answered any way you like? Is air superiority more difficult to achieve when our war objective is an armistice on favorable terms instead of victory? The question is one of air superiority in limited war. Is it possible? Does it put specific constraints on us? Should it be conceived in a wholly different manner?

Momyer: I will be glad to tackle it with my view. Again I don't think you can generalize. Sanctuaries in Korea, for example, didn't bother us particularly because of the limited objective of the enemy's force. The sanctuaries, insofar as the air superiority mission in Vietnam was concerned, didn't bother us too much either. So for that particular scenario, you could say that you had air superiority in two aspects: one of containment and the other by virtue of default. He didn't challenge you.

You accomplished the basic purpose that you were trying to achieve. You gave your ground forces and naval forces freedom of action without interference. So you accomplished the basic purpose of air superiority. On the other hand, if you postulate a situation where he has got a significant size air force and he operates that air from sanctuaries and he is willing to use that air against your facilities and so forth, then you are confronted with an entirely different circumstance. If you can't go at his bases and he has complete freedom of operation to attack your bases, then you are forced into a position of attrition. And I am not sure you are going to win that kind of a battle. If you can't really win that kind of an air battle, it's questionable whether you can really continue to do ground and sea operations. So I think you have to look at the specific situation.

I would say that you really are confronted with a very difficult political situation. If he is conducting aggressive operations from a sanctuary and you can't go against it, I think every military commander at that point in time has got to step forward. Your objectives may have to be changed in that conflict. You may have to seek other means of settling it because your air is at a very distinct disadvantage. It is so fundamental to the conduct of the whole of the operation that if air can't do its job then your total military objective may be in question.

Lee: The question of air superiority would be true whether it was armistice or a victory objective. Do you agree with that?

Kohn: To turn the question around now in a different area, once lost how does one regain air superiority? I suppose it might depend on how one lost it.

Ferguson: And what you have left.

Momyer: Well, I can go back to a historical example. The British lost air superiority on the Western Desert for the simple reason that they didn't have enough forces left after the Battle of Britain to be able to deploy them to the Western Desert. As a consequence we were reequipping a lot of the British forces with American equipment. Fortunately you were able to be given the opportunity....

Ferguson: To call on your friends.

Momyer: Yes, that's right. To rebuild.

Quesada: Another possible solution is to hope for a Hitler, to be fighting a damn dummy, fighting somebody that has no concept of how to conduct a war, who has no confidence in his military establishment, who deprives them of the power of authority and advice. I think Germany lost the war because of Hitler. Because he didn't use any military advice or direction. So you can hope for a Hitler.

Momyer: You may not be given the opportunity or time to reconstruct. It depends on how he exploits.

Quesada: You know I am being facetious.

Kohn: I think you also have an essential point: the mistakes that Hitler made that you mentioned in the Battle of Britain.

Momyer: But that's really a tough question if you are trying to contain and not escalate into a nuclear war. Suppose you get major forces involved. You can think in terms of scenarios in Southwest Asia, but this gets really very difficult if you are confronted with Soviet forces operating from sanctuaries in the Soviet Union. Whether you could really hold the air under those circumstances is very questionable.

Kohn: Let me ask one last question. If you had to isolate a single most critical factor in gaining and holding air superiority, trying to generalize— as difficult as I know it is—across time, three different wars, your own experiences, and different kinds of situations, what would you say?

Momyer: I don't think you can sum it up in a single statement. I think that's the difficulty. I don't think you can generalize to that extent, really.

Kohn: Then perhaps what you are saying is that you must be flexible; you must be prepared, as General Ferguson said, to get the map and find out where you are and look at the forces.

Momyer: I think you could say in essence that, philosophically, air superiority is essential to the operation of all military forces and your air has got to be responsive to whatever the political dictates are of the situation in which you are engaged. Your air power must be able to engage a wide variety of target systems. I guess, in a bottom-line statement, I would say there is absolute necessity for a single air component commander who has the authority to employ air in accordance with whatever the political situation demands.

Lee: I would like to say that, when this is being reviewed, somebody should go back and seek out the original copy of [Field Manual] 100–20 which was written in the Pentagon, I think. I don't know whether it would be indicated as being authored by Brig. Gen. Ralph Stearley or his commit-tee, but you will find that it is based on the type of operations philosophy that "Maori" Coningham practiced. In there will be pretty much what the current philosophy and doctrine of the Air Force is today, probably ex-panded upon a bit now from various and sundry experience. I would like to see it myself after this discussion here to see what it says, because I had forgotten about it. It's in there. It would be very interesting.

Quesada: May I make a suggestion to you all as historians? As I reflect on the conversation here, we seem to have focused on what made us win. It might serve a useful purpose if some historical effort were made to determine in a historic way what made Hitler lose. I think there are some good lessons to be learned, to note his errors. They were very cardinal errors. It might be helpful to us.

Momyer: We might do a little analysis on what we did wrong. We spend most of our time really patting ourselves on the back about how well we did. But we really never got in to analyze what we really did wrong, very little.

Quesada: We are such incredible innovators that we overcame our errors almost without recognizing them.

Kohn: Let me thank you greatly for your time, your thoughts, and your effort here today. So many of the things you have raised and discussed support an old adage: "The more things change, the more they stay the same." The problems of employing air power and of the use of air forces in war recur, although perhaps not always in the same exact way. Time again these same essential issues and themes have come forward over forty years. My suspicion is that they will come forward over the next forty years and beyond.

Quesada: Are you tracking as carefully as is possible what is going on in Israel and the Middle East where people are using some of our more advanced aircraft, F–15, F–16, and so forth?

Kohn: I believe the Air Staff is and the Air Force....

Ferguson: That's not history yet.

Kohn: That's not history yet, General Ferguson, but I am assured that they are.

Quesada: As the "junior officer" here, you young squirts, let me thank you on behalf of all of us for the opportunity to not only to get together ourselves but to sound off and discuss these problems with you. We hope it has been helpful.

Kohn: We think it has been very helpful. Thank you all once again.

Interview participants: (l. to r.) Gen. Robert M. Lee, Dr. Richard H. Kohn (moderator), Gen. James Ferguson, Lt. Gen. Elwood R. Quesada, and Gen. William W. Momyer.

Appendix

WAR DEPARTMENT FIELD MANUAL
FM 100-20

COMMAND

AND EMPLOYMENT

OF AIR POWER

WAR DEPARTMENT   •   21 JULY 1943

United States Government Printing Office
Washington : 1944

TABLE OF CONTENTS

WAR DEPARTMENT,
WASHINGTON 25, D. C., 21 July 1943.

FM 100–20, Field Service Regulations, Command and Employment of Air Power, is published for the information and guidance of all concerned.

[A. G. 300.7 (30 Jun 43).]

BY ORDER OF THE SECRETARY OF WAR:

G. C. MARSHALL,
Chief of Staff.

OFFICIAL:

J. A. ULIO,
Major General,
The Adjutant General.

DISTRIBUTION:

Bn and H 1 (8), 2–55 (5).

(For explanation of symbols see FM 21–6.)

FIELD SERVICE REGULATIONS

COMMAND AND EMPLOYMENT OF AIR POWER

(This manual supersedes FM 1–5, 18 January 1943. Pending revision of existing War Department publications which are affected by the publication of FM 100–20, whenever their contents are in conflict with the provisions of this manual, these instructions will govern.)

CHAPTER 1

GENERAL

SECTION I

DOCTRINE OF COMMAND AND EMPLOYMENT

■ 1. RELATIONSHIP OF FORCES.—LAND POWER AND AIR POWER ARE CO-EQUAL AND INTERDEPENDENT FORCES; NEITHER IS AN AUXILIARY OF THE OTHER.

■ 2. DOCTRINE OF EMPLOYMENT.—THE GAINING OF AIR SUPERIORITY IS THE FIRST REQUIREMENT FOR THE SUCCESS OF ANY MAJOR LAND OPERATION. AIR FORCES MAY BE PROPERLY AND PROFITABLY EMPLOYED AGAINST ENEMY SEA POWER, LAND POWER, AND AIR POWER. HOWEVER, LAND FORCES OPERATING WITHOUT AIR SUPERIORITY MUST TAKE SUCH EXTENSIVE SECURITY MEASURES AGAINST HOSTILE AIR ATTACK THAT THEIR MOBILITY AND ABILITY TO DEFEAT THE ENEMY LAND FORCEES ARE GREATLY REDUCED. THEREFORE, AIR FORCES MUST BE EMPLOYED PRIMARILY AGAINST THE ENEMY'S AIR FORCES UNTIL AIR SUPERIORITY IS OBTAINED. IN THIS WAY ONLY CAN DESTRUCTIVE AND DEMORALIZING AIR ATTACKS AGAINST LAND FORCES BE MINIMIZED AND THE INHERENT MOBILITY OF MODERN LAND AND AIR FORCES BE EXPLOITED TO THE FULLEST.

■ 3. COMMAND OF AIR POWER.—THE INHERENT FLEXIBILITY OF AIR POWER, IS ITS GREATEST ASSET. THIS FLEXIBILITY MAKES IT POSSIBLE TO EMPLOY THE WHOLE WEIGHT OF THE AVAILABLE AIR POWER AGAINST SELECTED AREAS IN TURN; SUCH CONCENTRATED USE OF THE AIR STRIKING FORCE IS A BATTLE WINNING FACTOR OF THE FIRST IMPORTANCE. CONTROL OF AVAILABLE AIR POWER MUST BE CENTRALIZED AND COMMAND MUST BE EXERCISED THROUGH THE AIR FORCE COMMANDER IF THIS INHERENT FLEXIBILITY AND ABILITY TO DELIVER A DECISIVE BLOW ARE TO BE FULLY EXPLOITED. THEREFORE, THE COMMAND OF AIR AND GROUND FORCES IN A THEATER OF OPERATIONS WILL BE VESTED IN THE SUPERIOR COMMANDER CHARGED WITH THE ACTUAL CONDUCT OF OPERATIONS IN THE THEATER, WHO WILL EXERCISE COMMAND OF AIR FORCES THROUGH THE AIR FORCE COMMANDER AND COMMAND OF GROUND FORCES THROUGH THE GROUND FORCE COMMANDER. THE SUPERIOR COMMANDER WILL NOT ATTACH ARMY AIR FORCES TO UNITS OF THE GROUND FORCES UNDER HIS COMMAND EXCEPT WHEN SUCH GROUND FORCE UNITS ARE OPERATING INDEPENDENTLY OR ARE ISOLATED BY DISTANCE OR LACK OF COMMUNICATION.

SECTION II

MILITARY AVIATION

■ 4. GENERAL CATEGORIES.—Aviation of the United States Army, referred to herein as military aviation, falls into two general categories as follows:

    a. Aviation directly under command and control of the Commanding General, Army Air Forces. Included in this category are—

    (1) All nontactical elements of the Army Air Forces such as those used for training, research, development, test, procurement, storage, issue, maintenance, and transport.

    (2) All tactical units of the Army Air Forces not assigned to a theater or task force Commander.

b. Aviation directly under command and control of other commanders. (The Commanding General, Army Air Forces, has such technical command of this aviation as is necessary for the control and supervision of training and the supply and maintenance of equipment peculiar to the Army Air Forces.) This category consists of air forces assigned to theater or task force commanders.

■ **5. TYPES OF TACTICAL AVIATION.**—In accordance with the purpose for which various types of aircraft are ordinarily employed, tactical aviation is organized, trained, and equipped to engage in offensive and defensive air operations. Corresponding to the means with which equipped, tactical aviation is divided into bombardment, fighter, reconnaissance, photographic, and troop-carrier aviation.

a. Bombardment aviation is the term applied to all aircraft designed for the air attack of surface objectives, and the organizations equipped with such aircraft.

b. Fighter aviation is the term applied to all aircraft designed for offensive air fighting, and the organizations equipped with such aircraft. (Fighter-bomber aircraft are fighters modified so that they may attack surface objectives.)

c. Reconnaissance aviation is the term applied to air units which perform the service of information for military commands. The function of reconnaissance aviation is to secure information by visual and photographic means and to return this information for exploitation.

d. Photographic aviation is the term applied to air units which perform photographic reconnaissance missions beyond the responsibilities or capabilities of reconnaissance aviation and special photogrammetric mapping missions for engineer topographic troops.

e. Troop carrier (including gliders) is the term applied to air units which carry parachute troops, airborne troops, and cargo.

f. The tactics and technique of performing the functions of air attack, air fighting, and air reconnaissance are set forth in FM1-10, 1-15, and 1-20. Communication procedure essential to air force operations is contained in FM 31-35 and FM 1-45.

3

SECTION III

ORGANIZATION

■ 6. IN A THEATER OF OPERATIONS.—In a theater of operations, there will normally be one air force. This air force will be organized in accordance with the task it is required to perform in any particular theater and, therefore, no set organization of an air force can be prescribed. However, the normal composition of an air force includes a strategic air force, a tactical air force, an air defense command, and an air service command. An air force may also include troop carrier and photographic aviation.

■ 7. OF AVIATION UNITS.—a. Tactical air units of the Army Air Forces from the smallest to the largest are designated flight, squadron, group, wing, division, command, and air force. The method of assignment and employment of the air forces necessitates a highly flexible organization within tactical units.

b. (1) The flight is the basic tactical grouping or unit of the Army Air Forces and consists of two or more airplanes.

(2) The squadron is the basic administrative and tactical unit and consists of three or four flights, depending upon the type of aviation.

(3) The group, composed of three or more squadrons, is both tactical and administrative; it contains all the elements essential for its air operations.

(4) The wing is the next higher unit of the Army Air Forces and its functions are primarily tactical.

(5) Two or more wings may be combined to form an air division.

(6) An "air command" may include divisions, wings, groups, service and auxiliary units, and is both tactical and administrative.

(7) The air force is the largest tactical unit of the Army Air Forces. It may contain a strategic air force, a tactical air force, an air defense command, and an air service command. It requires aviation engineer units for the construction and maintenance of air bases.

c. Units are designated according to their primary functions; for example, reconnaissance squadron, fighter group, bomber wing, air service command.

d. Ordinarily the group is the largest unit of the Army Air Forces that will operate in the air as a tactical entity under the command of one individual. Many air operations are conducted by smaller units. Reconnaissance and photographic missions, and less frequently bombardment missions, may be carried out by single airplanes with the required fighter cover.

e. In addiiton to tactical units, units are organized for the purpose of maintenance and supply and for facilitating air operations. These units comprise personnel of the Army Air Forces and Army Service Forces who are trained for rendering service for the Army Air Forces. The maintenance and service units serving an air force are collectively designated the air service command.

CHAPTER 2

AIR OPERATIONS

SECTION I

GENERAL

■ 8. BASIC TASKS.—The combat operations in which air force units are engaged are directed toward the accomplishment of the following basic tasks:

  a. Destroy hostile air forces. This will be accomplished by attacks against aircraft in the air and on the ground, and against those enemy installations which he requires for the application of air power.

  b. Deny the establishment and destroy existing hostile bases from which an enemy can conduct operations on land, sea, or in the air.

  c. Operate against hostile land or sea forces, the location and strength of which are such as to threaten the vital interests of the United States or its Allies.

  d. Wage offensive air warfare against the sources of strength, military and economic, of the enemies of the United States and its Allies, in the furtherance of approved war policies.

  e. Operate as a part of the task forces in the conduct of military operations.

  f. Operate in conjunction with or in lieu of naval forces.

■ 9. BASIC DOCTRINE OF EMPLOYMENT.—a. A knowledge of the powers and limitations of military aviation is a prerequisite to sound employment. Air operations almost invariably precede the contact of surface forces. The orderly mobilization and strategic concentration of the field forces and their ability to advance from their concentration areas in accordance with the strategical plan of operations depend in large measure on the success of these early air operations.

b. Air operations in joint Army and Navy operations are undertaken in furtherance of the strategical and tactical plan. They include the air operations for which the Army is responsible under special regulations governing joint action of the Army and the Navy. The success of such air operations can be assured only by adequate joint training and careful joint planning.

c. Complete control of the air can be gained and maintained only by total destruction of the enemy's aviation. Since this is seldom practicable, counter air force operations in the theater must be carried on continuously and intensively to gain and maintain air supremacy and to provide security from hostile air operations.

d. The impracticability of gaining complete control of the air necessitates the constant maintenance of air defenses to limit the effectiveness of enemy air operations.

e. In order to obtain flexibility, the operations of the constituent units of a large air force must be closely coordinated. Flexibility enables air power to be switched quickly from one objective to another in the theater of operations. Control of available air power in the theater must be centralized and command must be exercised through the air force commander.

f. Experience in combat theaters has proved the requirement for centralized control, by the air commander, of reconnaissance aviation as well as other types of aviation. Reconnaissance missions must be closely coordinated with our own fighter activities and are directly influenced by hostile fighter action. The attachment of a reconnaissance unit to the corps or smaller ground unit would deprive that reconnaissance unit of essential operating information and fighter protection which are readily available to the air commander only. The information of hostile air activities gained by the aircraft warning service will be furnished by the air commander to missions prior to take-off; and when urgent, to the reconnaissance unit in the air. This centralized control improves operating efficiency of reconnaissance aviation and limits reconnaissance losses. The Army Air Forces is responsible for providing the reconnaissance and photographic missions essential to the success of the ground forces in each theater of operations. The absence of reconnaissance units specially trained and equipped for the performance of such missions does not alter this responsibility.

g. When task forces are formed because of isolation by distance or lack of communication, the doctrine of command still applies (sec. I, ch. 1). The task force commander will command his ground forces through a ground force commander and his air force through an air commander.

■ 10. AIR BASES.—Air bases, suitably located, are essential for the sustained operation of military aviation.

a. Much of the equipment pertaining to aircraft is of a complex and highly technical nature; its operation requires highly trained air crews; its maintenance and repair require mechanics with specialized skill. All aircraft need regular and frequent care and maintenance. They are vulnerable to air attack both in flight and on the ground. The fatigue of air crews and the repair and reservicing of equipment and material require all aviation units to operate from air bases where the necessary facilities are provided for security, rest, replacement, maintenance, and repair.

b. The essential requirements for base facilities are landing areas, facilities for tactical control and planning, administration, maintenance, repair and supply, and provisions for the security of personnel and equipment on the ground. Aviation engineers are essential for the construction and maintenance of air bases. Adequate communications for the control and direction of air operations and for liaison are required.

SECTION II

STRATEGIC AIR FORCE

■ 11. GENERAL.—Strategic air force operations are undertaken in furtherance of the strategic plans prepared by the War Department General Staff. The selection of strategic objectives is a responsibility of the theater commander. Ordinarily, the theater commander will control these air operations by the assignment of a broad general mission to the air force commander. The air force commander executes the assignment by means of a directive to the strategic air force commander and general supervision of his forces.

■ 12. MISSIONS.—Generally, the aim of the strategic air force is the defeat of the enemy nation. Missions are selected which make a maximum contribution to this aim. Objectives may be found in the vital centers in the enemy's lines of communication and important establishments in the economic system of the hostile country. Objectives are selected in accordance with the ultimate purpose of the strategic plan. Counter air force operations necessary to neutralize or limit the power of the enemy's air forces are of continuing importance. Although normally employed against objectives listed above, when the action is vital and decisive, the strategic air force may be joined with the tactical air force and assigned tactical air force objectives.

■ 13. COMPOSITION.—The strategic air force is normally comprised of heavy bombardment, fighter, and photographic aviation. Heavy bombardment aviation is the backbone of the strategic air force. This class of aviation is characterized by its ability to carry heavy loads of destructive agents for great distances. It is also capable of conducting long-range strategic reconnaissance over land and sea. It relies upon speed, altitude, defensive fire power, and armor for security. Accompanying fighter aviation, where its radius of action permits, is also used to increase security. Fighter aviation furnishes air defense for bombardment bases. Photographic aviation performs long range high altitude photographic missions for the theater, air force, and strategic air force commanders.

SECTION III

TACTICAL AIR FORCE

■ 14. GENERAL.—*a.* In a theater of operations where ground forces are operating, normally there will be a tactical air force. Modern battle strategy and tactics derive success to

9

the degree that air power, sustained and in mass, is employed properly by the theater or task force commander.

b. The decision to launch a combined operation and to wage subsequent offensives is strongly influenced by the quantity and quality of air strength available.

c. Forces must be developed and committed to battle with overwhelming air components opposing estimated enemy air capabilities.

d. Tactical air force operations and ground force operations in the theater or task force will be coordinated by means of timely planning conferences of pertinent commanders and staffs, and through the exchange of liaison officers. Air and ground liaison officers will be officers who are well versed in air and ground tactics.

e. In modern battle operations, the fighting of land elements and the general air effort in the theater must be closely coordinated. The air battle should be won first whenever other considerations permit (par. 2).

■ 15. COMPOSITION.—*a.* The tactical air force may contain the following: reconnaissance aviation, light and medium bombardment units, fighter aviation and an aircraft warning service. This force does not serve the ground forces only; it serves the theater. Aviation units must not be parceled out as the advantage of massed air action and flexibility will be lost.

b. In a particularly opportune situation (offensive) or a critical situation (defensive), a part or a whole of the strategic air force may be diverted to tactical air force missions.

■ 16. MISSIONS.—*a.* The mission of the tactical air force consists of three phases of operations in the following order of priority:

(1) *First priority.*—To gain the necessary degree of air superiority. This will be accomplished by attacks against aircraft in the air and on the ground, and against those enemy installations which he requires for the application of air power.

(2) *Second priority.*—To prevent the movement of hostile troops and supplies into the theater of operations or within the theater.

(3) *Third priority.*—To participate in a combined effort of the air and ground forces, in the battle area, to gain objectives on the immediate front of the ground forces.

b. (1) *First priority.*—The primary aim of the tactical air force is to obtain and maintain air superiority in the theater. The first prerequisite for the attainment of air supremacy is the establishment of a fighter defense and offense, including RDF (radio direction finder), GCI (ground control interception), and other types of radar equipment essential for the detection of enemy aircraft and control of our own. While our air superiority is maintained, both the ground forces and the air force can fight the battle with little interference by the enemy air. Without this air supremacy, the initiative passes to the enemy. Air superiority is best obtained by the attack on hostile airdromes, the destruction of aircraft at rest, and by fighter action in the air. This is much more effective than any attempt to furnish an umbrella of fighter aviation over our own troops. At most an air umbrella is prohibitively expensive and could be provided only over a small area for a brief period of time.

(2) *Second priority.*—The disruption of hostile lines of communication (and at times lines of signal communication), the destruction of supply dumps, installations, and the attack on hostile troop concentrations in rear areas will cause the enemy great damage and may decide the battle. This accomplishes the "isolation of the battlefield." If the hostile force is denied food, ammunition, and reenforcements, aggressive action on the part of our ground forces will cause him to retire and the immediate objective will be gained. Massed air action on these targets with well-timed exploitation by ground forces should turn the retirement into rout.

(3) *Third priority.*—The destruction of selected objectives in the battle area in furtherance of the combined air-ground effort, teamwork, mutual understanding, and cooperation are essential for the success of the combined effort in the battle area. In order to obtain the necessary close teamwork the command posts of the Tactical Air Force and of the ground force concerned should be adjacent or common, at least during this phase of operations. Air and ground commanders

profit greatly from the other's successes. Airplanes destroyed on an enemy airdrome and in the air can never attack our troops. The advance of ground troops often makes available new airdromes needed by the air force. Massed air action on the immediate front will pave the way for an advance. However, in the zone of contact, missions against hostile units are most difficult to control, are most expensive, and are, in general, least effective. Targets are small, well-dispersed, and difficult to locate. In addition, there is always a considerable chance of striking friendly forces due to errors in target designation, errors in navigation, or to the fluidity of the situation. Such missions must be against targets readily identified from the air, and must be controlled by phase lines, or bomb safety lines which are set up and rigidly adhered to by both ground and air units. Only at critical times are contact zone missions profitable.

SECTION IV

AIR DEFENSE COMMAND

■ 17. GENERAL.—*a*. Air defense is the direct defense against hostile air operations as distinguished from the indirect defense afforded by counter air force operations. Air defense comprises all other methods designed to prevent, to interfere with, or to reduce the effectiveness of hostile air action.

b. Air defense is divided into active air defense and passive air defense.

(1) Active air defense comprises all measures aimed to destroy or to threaten destruction of hostile aircraft and their crews in the air. Active air defense is provided by fighter aircraft, antiaircraft artillery, and small arms fire; and by obstacles, principally barrage balloons

(2) Passive air defense is provided by dispersion, camouflage, blackouts, and other measures which minimize the effect of hostile air attack.

■ 18. COMPOSITION.—*a*. The active air defense means for any area may include fighter aviation, antiaircraft artillery, searchlights, barrage balloons and aircraft warning service.

Areas of responsibility for active air defense will be prescribed by the air force commander. Normally, the tactical air force will be responsible for the active air defense of the battle area utilizing fighter aircraft and the mobile aircraft warning service. This mobile aircraft warning service will include RDF (radio direction finder), GCI (ground control interception), and other types of radio equipment and warning facilities essential for the interception of enemy aircraft.

b. When antiaircraft artillery, searchlights, and barrage balloons operate in the air defense of the same area with aviation, the efficient exploitation of the special capabilities of each, and the avoidance of unnecessary losses to friendly aviation, demand that all be placed under the command of the air commander responsible for the area. This must be done.

c. Antiaircraft artillery attached or assigned to ground forces combat units remain under the command of the ground force unit commander, as distinguished from the antiaircraft units assigned to an air commander for the air defense of an area.

■ 19. TACTICS AND TECHNIQUE.—Tactics and technique of air operations in air defense are covered in FM 1–15.

SECTION V

AIR SERVICE COMMAND

■ 20. GENERAL.—The air service command in a theater provides the logistical framework of the air force. Its functions comprise such activities as procurement, supply, repair, reclamation, construction, transportation, salvage, and other services required by the tactical units of an air force. The air service command provides all repair and maintenance of equipment beyond the responsibility of first and second echelons of maintenance.

■ 21. ORGANIZATION.—*a.* All air force service organizations and installations are under the air service commander's direct control. These organizations and installations include air quartermaster, ordnance, signal, chemical, medical, and engineer depots, and service centers. Where ground force depots supplying material *common to both ground and air forces* are adequate, suitably located, and can be used, such material should not be handled by an air force depot. Material peculiar to the Army Air Forces will normally be handled only by the Army Air Forces and not by ground or service force agencies.

b. The service center is a mobile organization provided to establish and operate the necessary third echelon maintenance, reclamation, and supply points within close supporting distance of the combat units. Service centers normally are set up on the basis of one for each two combat groups.

■ 22. REFERENCE.—The details of organization, functions, and method of operation of an air service command are contained in Army Air Forces Regulations 65–1.

○

Select Bibliography

Governmental Sources

Books and Studies

Appleman, Roy E. *South to the Naktong, North to the Yalu.* [U.S Army in the Korean War].
Washington: Office of the Chief of Military History, Department of the Army, 1961.

Chennault, Capt Claire L. Air Corps. *The Role of Defensive Pursuit.* Maxwell Field, Ala.: Air Corps
Tactical School, 1933.

Craven, Wesley F., and Cate, James L., eds. *The Army Air Forces in World II.* 7 vols. Chicago:
University of Chicago Press, 1948–58.

Field, James A., Jr. *History of United States Naval Operations: Korea.* Washington: Naval History
Division, 1962.

Finney, Robert T. *History of the Air Corps Tactical School, 1920–1940.* USAF Historical Study 100.
Maxwell Air Force Base, Ala.: USAF Historical Division, 1955.

Futrell, Robert F. *The United States Air Force in Korea, 1950–1953.* New York: Duell, Sloan and
Pearce, 1961.

Goldberg, Alfred, ed. *A History of the United States Air Force, 1907–1957.* Princeton, N.J.: D. Van
Nostrad Co, 1957.

Greer, Thomas H. *The Development of Air Doctrine in the Army Air Arm, 1917–1941.* USAF Historical
Study 89. Maxwell Air Force Base, Ala.: United States Air Force Historical Division, 1955.

Hewes, James E., Jr. *From Root to McNamara: Army Organization and Administration, 1900–1963.*
Washington: Center of Military History, United States Army, 1975.

Historical Branch, USMC. *United States Marine Operations in Korea, 1950–1953.* 5 vols. Washington: Historical Branch, United States Marine Corps, 1954–72.

Holley, Irving B., Jr. *Buying Aircraft: Materiel Procurement for the Army Air Forces.* [United States
Army in World War II, Special Studies]. Washington: Office of the Chief of Military History,
Department of the Army, 1964.

Matloff, Maurice, and Snell, Edwin M. *Strategic Planning for Coalition Warfare, 1941–1942.* [United
States Army in World War II, The War Department]. Washington: Office of the Chief of Military
History, Department of the Army, 1953.

Miller, Samuel D. *An Aerospace Bibliography.* Washington: Office of Air Force History, 1978.

Momyer, Gen William W., USAF, Ret. *Air Power in Three Wars (WW II, Korea, Vietnam).* Washington:
Government Printing Office, 1978.

Richards, Dennis, and Saunders, Hilary St. George. *Royal Air Force, 1939–1945.* 3 vols. London: Her
Majesty's Stationery Office, 1953–54.

Shiner, John F. *Foulois and the U.S. Army Air Corps, 1931–1935.* Washington: Office of Air Force
History, 1982.

Webster, Charles K., and Frankland, Noble. *The Strategic Air Offensive Against Germany, 1939–1945.*
4 vols. London: Her Majesty's Stationery Office, 1961.

Symposium

Air Power and Warfare. Proceedings of the 8th Military History Symposium, United States Air Force
Academy, October 18–20, 1978. Washington: Office of Air Force History and the United States
Air Force Academy, 1979.

Publications

Air Force Manual 1–1, *Functions and Basic Doctrine of the United States Air Force*. February 14, 1979.
War Department Field Manual 31–35, *Air-Ground Operations*. August 13, 1946.
War Department Field Manual 100–20, *Command and Employment of Air Power*. July 21, 1943.

Congress

Hearings before the Committee on Expenditures in the Executive Departments. House of Representatives. 78th Cong, 1st sess. Washington: Government Printing Office, 1947.

Non-Governmental Sources

Books

Ambrose, Stephen E. *The Supreme Commander: The War Years of Dwight David Eisenhower*. New York: Doubleday & Co, 1970.

Bidwell, Shelford, and Graham, Dominick. *Fire Power: British Army Weapons and Theories of War, 1904–1945*. Boston: George Allen & Unwin, 1982.

Blumenson, Martin, ed. *The Patton Papers*. 2 vols. Boston: Houghton Mifflin Co, 1972–74.

Borowski, Harry R. *A Hollow Threat: Strategic Air Power and Containment Before Korea*. Westport, Conn.: Greenwood Press, 1982.

Bradley, Omar N. *A Soldier's Story*. New York: Henry Holt & Co, 1951.

Brown, Anthony Cave. *Bodyguard of Lies*. New York: Harper & Row, 1975.

Calvocoressi, Peter. *Top Secret Ultra*. New York: Pantheon Books, 1981.

Calvocoressi, Peter, and Wint, Guy. *Total War: Causes and Courses of the Second World War*. London: Penguin Books, 1972.

Carver, Field Marshal Sir Michael, ed. *The War Lords: Military Commanders of the Twentieth Century*. Boston: Little, Brown & Co, 1976.

Chennault, Maj Gen Claire L., USAF, Ret. *Way of a Fighter: The Memoirs of Claire Lee Chennault*. G. P. Putnam's Sons, 1949.

Coffey, Thomas M. *HAP: The Story of the U.S. Air Force and the Man Who Built It, General Henry H. "Hap" Arnold*. New York: The Viking Press, 1982.

Copp, DeWitt S. *A Few Great Captains: The Men and Events that Shaped the Development of U.S. Air Power*. Garden City, N.Y.: Doubleday & Co, 1980.

_____. *Forged in Fire: Strategy and Decisions in the Airwar over Europe, 1940–45*. New York: Doubleday & Co, 1982.

Greenfield, Richard. *Ethiopia: A New Political History*. New York: Frederick A. Praeger, 1965.

Hamilton, Nigel. *Monty: The Making of a General, 1887–1942*. New York: McGraw–Hill Book Co, 1981.

Hansell, Haywood S., Jr. *The Air Plan That Defeated Hitler*. Atlanta, Ga.: Higgins–McArthur, Longino and Porter, 1972.

Haugland, Vern. *The Eagle Squadrons: Yanks in the RAF, 1940–1942*. New York: Ziff-Davis Flying Books, 1979.

Hewlett, Richard G., and Anderson, Oscar E., Jr. *A History of the United States Atomic Energy Commission. Volume I: The New World, 1939–1946*. University Park, Pa.: Pennsylvania State University Press, 1962.

Higham, Robin. *Air Power: A Concise History*. New York: St. Martin's Press, 1973.

Hinsley, Francis H., *et al. British Intelligence in the Second World War: Its Influence on Strategy and Operations*. 2 vols. London: Cambridge University Press, 1979–81.

Hurley, Alfred F. *Billy Mitchell: Crusader for Air Power*. 2d ed. Bloomington, Ind.: Indiana University Press, 1975.

Kenney, George C. *General Kenney Reports: A Personal History of the Pacific War*. New York: Duell, Sloan & Pearce, 1949.

Korb, Lawrence J. *The Joint Chiefs of Staff: The First Twenty–Five Years*. Bloomington, Ind.: Indiana University Press, 1976.

LeMay, Curtis E., and Kantor, MacKinlay. *Mission with LeMay: My Story*. New York: Doubleday & Co, 1965.

Lewin, Ronald. *The American Magic: Codes, Ciphers, and the Defeat of Japan*. New York: Farrar, Straus, Giroux, 1982.

_____. *Ultra Goes to War*. New York: McGraw-Hill Book Co, 1978.

Montgomery of Alamein, Bernard M. Montgomery. *A History of Warfare*. Cleveland: World Publishing Co, 1968.

Nalty, Bernard. *Men and Battle: Tigers Over Asia*. New York: E. P. Dutton & Co, 1978.

Overy, R. J. *The Air War, 1939–1945*. New York: Stein & Day, 1981.

Pogue, Forrest C. *George C. Marshall: Ordeal and Hope, 1939–1942*. New York: The Viking Press, 1966.

Potter, E. B. *Nimitz*. Annapolis, Md.: Naval Institute Press, 1976.

Rostow, W. W. *Pre-Invasion Bombing Strategy: General Eisenhower's Decision of 25 March 1944*. Austin, Tex.: University of Texas Press, 1981.

Rust, Kenn C. *The 9th Air Force in World War II*. Fallbrook, Calif.: Aero Publishers, 1967.

Schoenebaum, Eleanora W. *The Truman Years*. Political Profiles Series. New York: Facts on File, 1978.

Schratz, Paul R., ed. *Evolution of the American Military Establishment Since World War II*. Lexington, Va.: The George C. Marshall Research Foundation, 1978.

Sims, Edward H. *American Aces in Great Fighter Battles of World War II*. New York: Harper & Bros, 1958.

Smith, Denis M. *Mussolini's Roman Empire*. New York: Penguin Books, 1977.

Tedder, Lord Arthur. *With Prejudice: The War Memoirs of a Marshal of the Royal Air Force*. Boston: Little, Brown & Co, 1966.

Thomas, Hugh. *The Spanish Civil War*. rev ed. New York: Harper & Row, 1977.

Westmoreland, Gen William C., USA, Ret. *A Soldier Reports*. Garden City, N.Y.: Doubleday & Co, 1976.

Articles

Chidlaw, Benjamin W. "Continental Air Defense." *Ordnance* 39 (March–April 1955), 706–10.

Coningham, Sir Arthur. "The Development of Tactical Air Forces." *Journal of the United Services Institute* IX (1946), 211–227.

Jones, Gen David C., USAF. "Why the Joint Chiefs of Staff Must Change." *Armed Forces Journal* 119 (March 1982), 62–72.

Meyer, Gen Edward C., USA. "The JCS—How Much Reform is Needed?" *Armed Forces Journal* 119 (April 1982), 82–90.

Newspapers

New York Times, February 18, 25, and March 1, 5, 31, 1982.

Index

INDEX